ADVANCE PRAISE FOR

HOMEGROWN
HANDGATHERED

"This book is simply a beautiful work. Jordan Tony and Silvan Goddin have instilled their hearts and souls into a celebration of Mother Earth and the Plant Nations. Their reverence of Indigenous agricultural lifeways is inherent in this book and provides resources and education for the novice or veteran gardener. This book can make your life more healthy, sustainable, and full of beauty."

—TAYLOR KEEN, author of *Rediscovering Turtle Island: A First Peoples' Account of the Sacred Geography of America* and founder of SacredSeed.org

"When it comes to growing your own food, Jordan Tony and Silvan Goddin are the real deal. Their dedication and passion to living off the land show up in every page of this book! They have put their life's learnings into these pages. There's so much to learn by reading this book. They give you a guide to living a self-sustaining life at any level. You don't need five acres of land! They show you how much abundance you can create from a small backyard or even a community garden plot. I love their philosophy on living simply, and I can't tell you how much inspiration I've received from their videos online and now from this incredible book. I highly recommend this book to anyone trying to increase self-sufficiency and connection to the land."

—MIKE GREENFIELD, creator of Pro Home Cooks

"As a long-time follower of Jordan Tony and Silvan Goddin's journey, I've come to deeply admire their unwavering commitment to sustainable living, foraging, and organic gardening. Their ability to transform a garden into a complete source of nourishment is nothing short of remarkable. They've taught me and countless others how to make the most of every inch of garden space, turning it into a reliable and abundant source of food.

This book is a beautiful extension of everything they've shared online, a blend of wisdom, practical advice, and a heartfelt connection to nature. Whether you're a seasoned gardener or just starting out, their insights will empower you to live more sustainably, directly from your own garden. This book is an essential resource to deepen your connection with the earth and truly live off the land."

—MEAGAN LLOYD, creator of *Meg Grows Plants*

HOMEGROWN HANDGATHERED

The Complete Guide to Living Off Your Garden

Silvan Goddin and Jordan Tony

Countryman Press

An Imprint of W. W. Norton & Company
Independent Publishers Since 1923

This book is intended as a general information resource for people who want to grow their own food. The authors are not doctors, dieticians, or food scientists. Please pay careful attention to the directions about processing and storing different foods that you grow, including how long you can safely store different foods in different ways (e.g., in the fridge and/or in an airtight container). Any commercial products that the authors recommend in this book are ones that the authors personally like. You need to do your own research to find the ones that are best for you. Any URLs displayed in this book link or refer to websites that existed as of press time. The publisher is not responsible for, and should not be deemed to endorse or recommend, any website other than its own or any app or content that it did not create. The authors, also, are not responsible for any third-party material.

For information about permission to reproduce selections from this book, write to Permissions, Countryman Press, 500 Fifth Avenue, New York, NY 10110

For information about special discounts for bulk purchases, please contact W. W. Norton Special Sales at specialsales@wwnorton.com or 800-233-4830

Manufacturing by RRD Asia
Book design by Allison Chi
Production manager: Devon Zahn

Countryman Press
www.countrymanpress.com

An imprint of W. W. Norton & Company, Inc.
500 Fifth Avenue, New York, NY 10110
www.wwnorton.com

978-1-68268-922-6

1 2 3 4 5 6 7 8 9 0

To our parents, for all the home-cooked meals and days spent in the garden, and to all the growers who came before us and contributed their wisdom, experience, and passion toward keeping humanity well-fed.

CONTENTS

ACKNOWLEDGMENTS

The information in this book belongs to all of us, but none of us owns it. We put our experiences into words and took photographs, but gardening knowledge itself has no owners. Around the world, our ancestors developed these crops, growing techniques, and recipes over thousands of years, and we try to remember that often. If you bought this book to learn to grow your own food, chances are your family's gardening history was interrupted, but have no doubt, your ancestors grew food and likely contributed to the information in this book. We thank them for that.

We are both lucky to have learned the magic of growing food at a young age: harvesting vegetables with tiny hands and watching the seasons unfold with siblings in our parents' vegetable gardens. We are forever grateful to our parents for inoculating us with a love for the natural world and watching things grow. Over the years, as we developed as gardeners and dedicated more time to growing food, we each learned from countless gardening mentors, Indigenous culture-keepers, biology professors, and the plants in the garden themselves.

We grow our food in an industrial city, and we have fertile ground in which to plant crops only because of the dedication of community gardeners and organizations advocating to preserve growing space and protect it from development. This same story holds true around the world, and we are so thankful for the dedicated efforts of people who maintain the soil, water, and seeds that feed us all.

Finally, we want to acknowledge you! Taking on a challenge like growing your own food can feel very intimidating at first, no doubt about it. There's a lot to learn, especially if you're starting from square one. You *will* make mistakes and you *will* have garden failures, but each of those offers a lesson that will help you become an even better gardener. We're so thankful to have another person taking steps toward producing healthy food for our communities and protecting our earth. Welcome to the team.

Young Jordan harvesting beans

Young Silvan helping spread compost

INTRODUCTION

After a day in the garden, whether we're bringing in a harvest or doing something a little less glamorous, such as spreading compost or weeding, we often turn to each other with a knowing smile. "I'm so grateful for gardening," one of us says, and the other nods approvingly because we have both said it so many times. Growing food has brought so much joy, fulfillment, and sustenance to our lives that it feels silly to call it just a hobby.

We both grew up in families with vegetable gardens, so we both experienced the thrill of harvesting and eating homegrown produce at a young, impressionable age. We witnessed first-hand the empowering feeling of sowing a seed and guiding it to maturity, not to mention the delight of being outside with our hands in the soil. In college, we both studied biology, focusing on ecology and botany. We met while volunteering at a community garden just off campus and had our first conversation while harvesting a row of purple mustard greens. After we graduated, Jordan completed a yearlong organic farming apprenticeship, and we started our own vegetable farm on rented land in rural North Carolina. It was small by farm standards, just 1 acre, but we poured our passion and energy into it and scratched out a *very* modest income for a couple years by selling vegetables and fruits to our community. We had a strong market and good growing skills, but the margins of small-scale vegetable production are so slim that we both had to continue working day jobs to pay our bills. Silvan worked as a lab technician at a butterfly laboratory, studying the effect of climate change on invertebrates, and Jordan worked as a sustainability consultant in the recycling industry. That arrangement left us with little spare time for anything else.

After pausing our farming dreams and moving to Pittsburgh, Pennsylvania, to be closer to Jordan's family, our gardening space shrank considerably. Instead of an acre, complete with high tunnels and a borrowed tractor, we had a balcony and a 15-by-20-foot plot in a community garden next to the local park. Nevertheless, we were grateful to have any growing space at all and considered it a fun, new challenge. We set up a seed-starting station in the laundry room of our third-floor apartment and filled our community garden plot with as many plants as possible.

When trying to maximize the output of a limited growing space, we often lean on the scientific process of observation, experimentation, and repetition that we learned in college. Part of the fun of gardening is that it functions as a miniature ecosystem and laboratory, where every season offers a chance to try something new and observe the results. But we began to understand fully what it meant to be a part of that ecosystem only when we tried to live off the food exclusively from our garden.

In the spring of 2016, Jordan decided to try eating only food we grew in our gardens or foraged in the woods—for one week. At that time of year, our community garden plot had some kale, turnips, a handful of strawberries, and some tiny carrots. Long story short: Jordan lost a lot of weight and was very grumpy for seven days, but we developed an important new perspective on growing food. As market farmers, we always focused on the most lucrative crops, such as heirloom tomatoes, salad greens, and strawberries. It made sense for earning or saving money, but tomatoes, salad, and strawberries didn't cut it when it came to feeding our bodies.

The next season, with a new focus on using our gardens to sustain us, we changed the balance of our crops to reflect our actual diet, making space for plants full of protein, fat, and carbohydrates. We learned the best, most efficient staple crops to grow in small spaces as well as how to grow them together in ways that enhanced the soil and reduced time spent weeding, fertilizing, and watering. We took guidance and inspiration from the Indigenous peoples of the Americas, who cultivated amazing crops—including corn, beans, potatoes, and squash—as well as our own Middle Eastern and European ancestors, who cultivated nutrient-dense staples, such as chickpeas, cabbage, and beets.

This new way of gardening changed our entire lifestyle. We preserved more of our food, filling the pantry and freezer with fruits and vegetables to enjoy in the winter rather than shopping at the grocery store. We saved seeds so the beautiful heirloom varieties of flour corn, dry beans, squash, and chickpeas could adapt to our local conditions. We even formalized our personal challenge—which we now call our Living off the Land challenges—kicking them off each fall and improving every year to the point that we now go comfortably for months without eating store-bought food. As I write this sentence, we're three and a half months into our 2024 Living off the Land challenge. Aside from doing a bit more cooking lately, it feels pretty normal for us.

As we've learned over the years, you don't need to own a giant farm to grow your own food, and you certainly don't need a trust fund. We have a yard of less than an eighth of an acre on a steep Pittsburgh slope. Along with some rented community garden plots we share with friends and family, we comfortably sustain ourselves for months on homegrown produce. As long as you have access to some ground or growing containers, you just need curiosity, passion, and the confidence to start. Remember to give yourself grace—don't expect to master growing everything in this book immediately or to implement all the techniques we suggest. Growing your own food is a lifelong journey, and we still learn new things every year, which we find to be one of the most exciting parts of this lifestyle! Don't forget that, above any book, video series, or mentor, your own experience from mistakes made in previous growing seasons will serve as your best teacher.

For easy reference, we've split this book into two parts. The first section covers general topics, such as planning your garden, companion planting, composting, managing pests, saving seeds, and more. In the second half, we cover the 16 crops we consider to be the most important for living off your garden. In each crop chapter, we detail how to grow, harvest, preserve, and cook with these incredible plants and mushrooms sustainably. As you add to your garden, refer to those pages for advice on how to cultivate and care for your crops. In the years to come, we hope the pages of this book become worn and stained with your soil-covered fingerprints. Above all, we hope you find as much joy and satisfaction in growing your own food as we do!

WHY GROW FOOD?

The bulk of this book explains how to grow your own food, but if you're like us, you probably also like to consider *why*. Ask 10 gardeners why they grow their own food, and you will likely get 10 different answers, running the gamut from "I'm preparing for the zombie apocalypse!" to "It brings me joy." One of those reasons seems a little healthier than the other, but once you start growing your own food, the benefits abound regardless of initial motivation.

We met in a community garden more than a decade ago and immediately hit it off. While harvesting a bed of mustard greens, we chatted about our love of gardening, dogs, and long hikes in the woods. Of course we shared a love for growing food, but through that conversation about *why* we loved growing food we discovered that we had similar values and passions. For us, growing food is important for our physical and mental health, building community, empowering one another, and living more in balance with our ecosystem. These themes appear throughout the book, but here's a primer on why we believe gardening supports personal health, community health, and ecosystem health.

Personal Health

Gardening offers an excellent low-impact exercise for people of all ages. It gets your muscles moving and your heart pumping. But unlike walking on a treadmill, bored to tears in front of a row of TVs at the gym, you don't even realize you're exercising. We don't consider counting calories a great way to monitor your health, but as a metric for physical exertion, an hour working in the garden uses about the same number of calories as running on a treadmill for half an hour.

Working in a garden also benefits your mental health. According to recent studies, contact with the soil bacteria *Mycobacterium vaccae* can significantly increase serotonin levels in the brain. Simply put, touching dirt makes us happy! This research forms part of a growing body of evidence that spending time around soil, plants, and wildlife can improve mental health, not just from the joy of being in nature but also through physical, chemical reactions.[1]

Working the soil in a garden can provide substantial health benefits, but the primary advantage of growing your own food comes from the bounty of produce you'll use to nourish yourself. If you have regular access to fresh produce at your local grocery store, that's a blessing. That said, most of the commercial crops produced for retail sale are bred and grown with three qualities in mind: pest and disease resistance, shipping quality, and shelf life. None of those attributes has anything to do with nourishment or flavor.

Many heirloom varieties of fruits and vegetables that our ancestors bred and ate for hundreds or thousands of years are especially delicious and nutrient-rich. Unfortunately, when packed into crates and thrown onto tractor trailers, many of

---

1   https://www.colorado.edu/today/2019/05/09/natures-original-stress-buster

these heirlooms turn to mush. At the turn of the 20th century, food became a global commodity and farmers started shipping their produce to centralized markets around the world. Instead of continuing the tradition of breeding crops that tasted the best or contained the most nutrition, they bred for traits such as appearing fresh after sitting in a distribution center for a week. Luckily for us, gardeners and small farmers around the world continued growing heirloom varieties to feed their communities, so seeds for these heritage varieties survived the shift to industrial agriculture. Every year, more gardeners and small farmers are cultivating these old varieties, meaning that some heirlooms are grown more widely now than ever before. In each of the specific crop chapters in Part Two, we highlight some of our favorite heirloom varieties, and, in the Seed Saving chapter (page 51), we cover breeding and maintaining your very own heirlooms.

Beyond choosing what varieties to grow, you can also improve the flavor and nutrition of your produce by harvesting it at optimal ripeness. For most produce grown for retail sale, commercial growers harvest it when slightly underripe to extend its shelf life. It either ripens after the fact in a warehouse or simply goes into stores in its anemic, underripe form. With homegrown produce, we don't have to worry about shipping, so we can pick perfectly soft, juicy tomatoes right off the vine and carry them straight to our kitchen!

Community Health

Many communities have little or no access to fresh produce. It's not as profitable for corporate supermarket chains to open locations in poor urban and rural areas so they simply don't. That profit strategy creates a patchwork of communities in which, if you don't own a vehicle, your options for feeding yourself and your family dwindle to fast-food chains or the dollar store. In many of these areas, people also lack access to land, so growing their own food isn't as simple as digging up a lawn. As a solution to this problem, public community gardening has been growing in popularity.

Community gardens come in a few different styles. Community groups often organize them on unused public land or vacant city lots. Some of these gardens are broken into individual plots in which each family or group can grow its own food. In others, the community works together to grow the food and then distributes it. In Pittsburgh we belong to two community gardens that not only have allowed us to produce a significant amount of our own food in an urban environment but also have helped us make invaluable connections with other like-minded folks with whom we share seeds, produce, and knowledge. When people find out that we grow most of our own food in little, rented, community garden plots rather than a big, rural farmstead, they are often taken aback—but that's nothing new.

At the start of World War II, farms suffered from labor shortages and the war effort shipped critical food supplies to soldiers overseas. Government agencies encouraged people to plant gardens and distributed seeds and pamphlets on how to grow food to avoid a famine on the home front. People with growing experience helped train others to work the land. Some estimates indicate that, by 1944, about 40 percent of all fruits and vegetables consumed in the United States came from victory gardens. Some of these gardens took root on public land, and various communities still use them to grow food to this day.

The American Community Gardening Association (communitygarden.org) has contact information for community garden managers around the world. If you don't have one in your area, consider organizing your own!

Ecosystem Health

Picture a typical modern farm. You are probably imagining a cornfield running in neat, straight rows in every direction as far as the eye can see. It may look like a computer planted it because one likely did. Massive tractors that cost hundreds of thousands of dollars use GPS to navigate fields while dragging precision seed drills that plant corn seed with pinpoint accuracy. With each seed, the tractors inject synthetic fertilizer to help the corn take hold in barren soil. The corn grows into flawless green stalks, seemingly untouched by insects because they drop dead after eating only a few bites. Runoff from synthetic fertilizer causes environmental devastation downstream. Regular applications of harsh pesticides and fungicides grind wildlife to a halt throughout the farm. Diesel-powered machinery pumps soot and greenhouse gases into the atmosphere. At the end of the season, the corn dries down until another implement on the massive tractor can scoop it up and pile it high in a tractor trailer that will deliver it for sale as animal feed. This story—massive ecological "dead zones" calibrated precisely to produce one crop and nothing else—applies to the vast majority of modern farmland. The term often used to describe this style of growing food is "factory farming."

Now picture a typical modern vegetable garden or small farm. You probably see a colorful array of diverse crops and flowers, with butterflies and bees fluttering from plant to plant. Maybe a gardener is inspecting a leaf with reverence. Growers plant crops by hand and fertilize them with compost generated from the previous year's garden waste. Cornstalks grow tall, adorned with climbing beans. Beneath them, sprawling winter squash cover the ground. The soil holding their intertwined roots teems with insects, worms, fungi, and beneficial bacteria. Beyond the obvious advantage that a well-managed garden provides a friendly habitat for native organisms, growing food this way has a host of other environmental benefits.

The EPA estimates that 11 percent of all carbon emissions come from industrial agriculture, much of that is the result of the massive, diesel-powered machines working the land. Additionally, 29 percent of carbon emissions come from transportation and another 30 percent from industrial manufacturing. Growing your own food cuts the need for any industrial manufacturing or transportation to put calories in your body. It also eliminates emissions from growing food almost entirely, since much of the work is done by hand (unless your vegetable garden contains lots of carbon-intensive infrastructure, such as concrete pathways, short-lived raised beds, and irrigation piping).[2]

The EPA also estimates that 30 to 40 percent of all food grown in the United States goes to waste. This disheartening process starts on mega-farms during the industrial harvesting, processing, and storage of produce. Some of that produce sustains damage or simply rots in the field. More food goes to waste as trucks transport it over long distances to distribution centers, which then transfer it to smaller trucks that transport it to grocery stores. On retail shelves some of it continues to spoil, and much of it ends up in grocery store dumpsters, from which yet another truck drags it away to rot in landfills. You can reduce or eliminate food waste by growing what you love

---

2   https://www.epa.gov/ghgemissions/sources-greenhouse-gas-emissions

to eat, harvesting it by hand at peak ripeness, and—if your garden gives you more than you can use when fresh—preserving the bounty or sharing with friends.

Growing your own food also significantly reduces waste beyond just rotting vegetables. The average home's trash or recycling bin contains a jumble of plastic bags, plastic tubs and lids, paper boxes and bags, much of it related directly to food. Jordan worked as a sustainability consultant in the waste industry for eight years and participated in a series of waste composition studies. In them, a bunch of waste experts tore open anonymous people's garbage on a big table before meticulously categorizing and weighing it. In every one of these studies, the vast majority of household garbage came from food packaging or food waste. When we do our annual Living off the Land challenge, seeing how long we can go without buying any food from the grocery store, we only need to put out our garbage bin about once per month. When not doing the challenge, we normally have to put it out every other week.

Growing food by hand also creates a direct, tangible connection between us and our environment. We all are connected to it—inextricably and at all times—regardless of whether we know it, but buying food grown on a distant farm and processed and packaged thousands of miles away distorts that connection. Alternatively, walking through a little ecosystem that you're helping to steward, surrounded by plants and fungi that produce the food fueling your body, creates a powerful feeling that has the potential to change your entire worldview.

LIVING OFF YOUR GARDEN

The first time Jordan attempted to eat only food we grew was an incredible learning experience because of how poorly it went. As small organic farmers, we sold our crops at local farmers' markets, focusing on high-demand fruits and vegetables, such as tomatoes, salad greens, spinach, and strawberries. Jordan quickly discovered those crops all contain low levels of the calories, fat, protein, and carbohydrates our bodies need to function. To say he was living off our garden during that first attempt is a bit of a stretch. More accurately, he was living off his stored body fat while periodically enjoying a bowl of raspberries or a plate of roasted radishes and kale. Since then, we have shifted our garden plan considerably. Now that we can make balanced meals, Silvan (who has more foresight) partakes in the annual challenge as well. We still enjoy our homegrown tomatoes and radishes, but when eating from our garden now, we use them as fixings on corn tortillas with black beans and roasted winter squash rather than as the main course.

Garden Planning for Balanced Meals

A balanced meal has enough calories and macronutrients to provide us with energy and enough micronutrients to keep our bodies functioning healthily. *Macro* just means "large-scale," and *micro* means "small-scale," so a balanced meal contains a lot of macronutrients—the protein, fat, and carbs in flour corn and black beans—and a smaller amount of micronutrients, such as the vitamins and minerals in a side of roasted carrots or spinach.

CALORIES

In American culture, the word *calorie* has become almost synonymous with *unhealthy*. For decades, processed food manufacturers advertised "healthy, low-calorie" foods to eat "guilt free!"—as though you ever should feel guilty about nourishing your body. In the world of growing your own food, calorie-dense crops are considered a blessing. Calories simply measure the amount of energy that food contains. Technically speaking, 1 calorie is the amount of energy it takes to raise the temperature of 1 gram of water by 1° Celsius. In human terms, your heart uses about 1 calorie for every 33 heartbeats.

Daily caloric requirements vary from person to person, depending on age, biological sex, and activity level. Adults generally require between 1,600 and 2,500 calories per day, which come from the carbohydrates, proteins, and fats in food. Your digestive system breaks these macronutrients apart, which releases energy your cells use to power everything from your heartbeat to your brain synapses processing the words on this page right now. Without calories, your body would completely cease to function, so from here on, the word *calorie* shouldn't represent something to avoid or restrict but, rather, the energy that keeps us alive and thriving.

MACRONUTRIENTS: CARBOHYDRATES, PROTEIN, FAT

We need these primary nutrients in great amounts to have energy, build muscle, and even think. Carbohydrates consist of various kinds of sugars and starches, the easiest forms of energy for our bodies to process. Each gram of carbohydrates has about 4 readily available calories. Eating a tablespoon of honey gives you an instant boost because your body can quickly transform that sugar into energy. Protein also serves as a good source of energy, but it mainly provides our bodies with amino acids, the building blocks for creating our own proteins. Each gram of protein has about 4 calories. Fat is also an important source of energy. It's a little harder to come by in garden crops, but each gram of fat has about 9 calories.

Growing Macronutrients

Staple crops—including flour corn, dry beans, chickpeas, potatoes, and winter squash—have lots of macronutrients. These crops form the base of a balanced diet and make us feel full after eating them. By weight, a typical dry flour corn contains about 75 percent carbohydrate, 10 percent protein, and 5 percent fat. If you're holding a 20-pound sack of dry corn, you're holding a full pound of fat! Our bodies need macronutrients in the greatest quantity, so we dedicate the bulk of the growing space in our community garden plots to these crops.

MICRONUTRIENTS: VITAMINS, MINERALS, PHYTOCHEMICALS

Micronutrients matter just as much as macronutrients, but our bodies need them in much smaller quantities to function optimally and stay healthy. Our bodies need vitamins to carry out everything from maintaining our immune system health to our bone integrity. In the absence of important vitamins, we don't starve like we do without calories, but we can develop debilitating diseases, including rickets, a bone disease caused by a vitamin D deficiency; scurvy, which develops from a lack of vitamin C; and pellagra, which results from a deficiency of vitamin B. Many vitamins also function as important antioxidants, which help protect our cells from the type of damage that can lead to various cancers.

Minerals similarly maintain our health. As any American inundated with those "Got milk?" ads as a child knows, "Calcium helps build strong bones!" The importance of minerals, such as calcium and iron, is well known, but a few industry groups have warped our understanding of how to consume them in order to sell more of their own products. Ask average Americans what foods contain calcium, and they will probably name only dairy products. Dairy products do contain calcium, but black beans and leafy greens, such as collards, kale, and spinach, are also packed with calcium! Food manufacturers often fortify processed foods with iron, another important mineral. Cereal companies may advertise their breakfast cereal as being the only source of dietary iron, but it naturally occurs in beans and grains in great amounts.

Phytochemicals are small micronutrients that provide many benefits to our bodies. Phytochemicals include things like carotenoids, polyphenols, and polysaccharides. According to the National Institutes of Health, "Phytochemicals possess strong antioxidant activities and exhibit antimicrobial, antidiarrheal, anthelmintic, antiallergic, antispasmodic, and antiviral activities." In a nutshell, they're good for you. *Phyto* means "plant" because these important compounds pri-

Micronutrient-rich peppers

marily come from the leaves, roots, and fruits of plants. Many phytochemicals are also found in mushrooms, but we won't hold it against whoever came up with that word.

Growing Micronutrients

Staple crops contain many micronutrients in addition to their macronutrients, but they pale in comparison with the vast array of fruits, veggies, and mushrooms in this book. Tomatoes, peppers, kale, collards, carrots, beets, shiitakes, and oyster mushrooms are not as calorie-dense as the staple crops mentioned previously, but what they lack in macronutrients they make up for in vitamins, minerals, and phytochemicals.

Leafy greens like kale, collards, and spinach are packed with calcium and vitamins A, C, E, and K, which help our organs and immune systems function properly. Other vegetables are full of phytochemicals that protect our cells by acting as antioxidants and neutralizing cancer-causing free radicals. Many phytochemicals, such as anthocyanins and carotenoids, are

colorful pigment molecules, which means we can actually see them in our food! Blue-purple anthocyanins occur in blueberries, blue corn, blue potatoes, purple carrots, purple peppers, and purple tomatoes. Orange-red carotenoids occur in carrots, pumpkins, red peppers, red tomatoes, sweet potatoes, and watermelon.

Mushrooms, including the shiitake and oyster varieties, contain ergothioneine, a powerful antioxidant. A review of 17 cancer studies from 1966 to 2020 by UCLA researchers suggested that eating just ⅛ cup of these mushrooms per day could lower your risk of cancer significantly.[3] Mushrooms grown outdoors or exposed to sunlight also provide a good source of vitamin D.

Our bodies need the critical micronutrients in fruits, veggies, and mushrooms in much smaller quantities than macronutrients, so we can grow a sufficient number of micronutrient-rich crops in a much smaller space than we dedicate to our staple crops.

Grow What You Like to Eat

In this chapter we've covered a lot of science, but don't forget that the purpose of your garden is to feed *you* (and the people you share with). If you want your garden to sustain you, you have to grow crops you like to eat. Black beans contain lots of protein and carbs, but they won't work as a staple crop if you hate eating them!

As you plan your garden, think of your favorite meals that contain crops that will grow in your area, then dedicate the biggest sections of your garden to those plants. Sitting down to a favorite meal made with ingredients you grew and harvested with your own hands not only fills your nutritional needs but also feeds your soul!

---

3   https://pubmed.ncbi.nlm.nih.gov/33724299/

PART ONE

GARDENING FOR SUSTENANCE

SITE SELECTION

Choosing the space for your garden might seem mundane, but location—more than a gardener's green thumb—often determines why some gardens succeed and others don't. Three critical elements will put your garden on the path to success.

Sunlight

The first and arguably most important point to consider is sunlight exposure. Plants need sun, and usually lots of it, to photosynthesize enough energy to feed themselves. If your growing space is a wide-open area with no trees or buildings to block the sun, you can disregard this section. (Also, we're jealous.) On the other hand, if buildings and trees surround your growing space, like ours, pay attention. Most vegetables and fruits require at least six hours of direct sunlight exposure to grow optimally. In the gardening world, we call this "full sun."

The simplest way to find the areas of your growing space that have full sun exposure is to wait for a sunny day during the growing season and take a picture of the area every two hours from when the sun touches the ground to when it leaves. Then look at the pictures to see which areas are receiving direct sunlight for at least six hours. Now you can narrow your potential garden location to those areas. Keep in mind that, if you monitor your sunlight when the sun hangs low in the sky in the dead of winter, you're dealing with far fewer sunlight hours than in the growing season.

If no part of your growing space receives six hours of sunlight, you still can grow a vegetable garden, but you'll want to focus more on leafy vegetables, such as kale, collards, and spinach, and less on fruiting crops, like tomatoes, pep-

pers, beans and corn. Also, if you have fewer than six hours of sunlight exposure, your yard might make a prime location for a mushroom garden.

Soil

Next, you'll want to examine the soil. We'll go into more detail about soil testing in the Soil Fertility and Nutrient Cycles chapter (page 23), but you're looking for uncompacted soil, free of contamination from heavy metals. That kind of contamination poses more of a concern in urban areas, like where we live. If you live in a city, we highly recommend testing your soil for lead. You can do that by digging a small sample, placing it in a sealable plastic bag, and mailing it to a soil laboratory that will test it and email you the results. Many agricultural universities provide this service to the public for a small fee.

You can mitigate lead-contaminated soil by adding tons of compost to dilute the contamination, but if your soil contains unsafe levels of lead, we recommend building a deep raised bed filled with compost and clean topsoil. Roots and low-lying leaves tend to absorb heavy metals at a much higher rate than fruiting crops, which filter out a lot of the lead before it makes its way to the fruit. Avoid growing root crops (e.g., carrots and beets) or short, leafy vegetables (e.g., spinach and lettuce) in lead-contaminated soil.

Uncompacted soil, also called tilthy soil, has air pockets that allow water, roots, and soil organisms to penetrate deep into it. If your soil feels rock-hard, you can amend it by digging it deeply with a broadfork, tilling it, and working in compost. After an initial tilling, you can maintain healthy, uncompacted soil through good growing practices which we'll discuss throughout this book.

Exposure to Animals

Now that you've found the sunniest spot in your growing space with the best soil, the final critical element to consider is exposure to critters. Look around and think about whether you might be planting a salad bar for local wildlife. Our neighborhood hosts deer, rabbits, groundhogs, squirrels, chipmunks, and more. Like most urban and suburban wildlife, they're bold. If you plant a crop they like and you don't protect it sufficiently, don't plan on harvesting much of it.

To protect your crops from hungry deer, a fence at least 6 feet and ideally 8 feet high around the entire garden offers the best deterrent. If you're only dealing with smaller critters, like rabbits and squirrels, chicken-wire fencing and row covers provide excellent deterrence. Accompany those barriers with a pet dog chasing them down every once in a while and they'll probably give up trying to eat your garden.

Finding the best location for your garden will save you a lot of heartache and labor later, so take time to explore your growing space before choosing where to plant your crops. But even in the worst-case scenario—a less-than-perfect location and a struggling garden—you can reconsider these conditions and choose a new location or different growing techniques the next season. It's better to start fresh with a sturdy foundation than to try to coax plants to grow in conditions for which they're not equipped.

EQUIPMENT

We're bare-bones gardeners and try to get by with as little stuff as possible. Our household MO is: "Don't buy anything, and if you need something, try to figure out a work-around first." That said, we've acquired a few tools over the years that have become so central to our food production and preservation that we don't know how we got by without them. These items by no means are must-haves, but they will make your life easier if-you-have.

In the Garden

HORI HORI: Pretty much every day in the planting season, you'll need a garden spade or something to dig little holes. Every garden spade we used bent or broke within a couple seasons—until we started using a hori hori. This sturdy tool, also known as a soil knife, is a Japanese invention originally designed to dig up roots in the country's mountainous terrain. It is incredibly sturdy and does an excellent job digging through even tough, compacted soil. It usually has measuring marks for easy plant spacing reference, and the serrated edge can cut through twine if you forget your scissors.

HOE: For bed prep early in the season and keeping weeds down in summer, a good hoe won't lack for work and will save your back from bending over to pull weeds. It's great for weeding because it destroys weeds at the soil surface but doesn't turn over the soil and expose weed seeds to conditions that will allow them to sprout. We also use hoes for covering furrows in which we've direct-seeded.

KNIFE: A knife can save you some mess at harvest time. You can rip many vegetables and fruits from the plant, but that occasionally damages the stalk and can reduce future harvests. Better to use a sharp knife to harvest.

TWINE: Twine is important for any crops that need to be trellised, such as tomatoes, peppers, peas, and beans. Most farm supply stores and seed companies sell big boxes of woven plastic tomato twine made for commercial tomato growers who are twining up acres of vegetables. For home gardeners, one of these boxes will last for years. Most local garden centers sell smaller rolls of biodegradable jute twine, which you can compost when done with it, but that kind generally doesn't have the same strength or lifespan as plastic twine.

PRUNERS: Sharp pruners work great for transitioning beds and cutting down plants. When it's time to remove your spring vegetables and plant summer crops, ripping out whole plants by the roots isn't ideal for all the mycorrhizal organisms living there. Cutting the plant at the soil line with pruners leaves the roots intact, which maintains soil health, creating a more hospitable environment for the next crop.

INSECT NETTING: Insect netting is our number one tool for keeping pests out of our leafy greens, ahead of pesticides, predatory insects, or hand-picking. Netting allows sunlight and water to reach your crops but prevents pest insects that wander through your yard from laying their eggs on your veggies.

BROADFORK: This implement looks pretty much how it sounds: a wide fork. It loosens soil in garden beds without inverting the layers like traditional tillage does. It also won't create a hardpan deep in the soil, which a tractor or tiller can over time. If you have heavy clay soils, using a broadfork in the spring can help create channels for your plants' roots to expand. Eventually, after building up the soil through mulching, cover cropping, and growing plants, you can likely phase out using the broadfork. At this point, we only use ours occasionally for crops that really appreciate loose soil, such as carrots and sweet potatoes.

SEEDLING TRAYS: You can use many kinds of containers—plastic cups, cartons, or even modified toilet paper rolls—to start your seeds as long as they are deep enough and you add drainage holes. However, once you go beyond starting a few plants, it's worth it to use dedicated seedling trays, which will allow you to water and transport your seedlings with minimal fuss. You can buy ones made of heavy-duty plastic that you can wash and reuse for many years. We use 72-cell trays for our larger seedlings that stay indoors longer before planting, including tomatoes, peppers, squash, and brassicas (kale, collards, cabbage), and 128-cell trays for crops like beans and squash, which we transplant soon after germination.

In soil blocking, an option gaining popularity, a small handheld press molds compost into blocks into which you sow your seeds directly, no container necessary. These use less or potentially zero plastic. You need to bottom-water them with a tray rather than using a watering can, and getting the right consistency of the soil mix so they hold their shape can be challenging. However, the lack of container walls allows the roots to "air prune"—rather than wrapping around themselves and potentially becoming root-bound—leading to seedlings that grow quickly once transplanted.

TRELLIS: Using the vertical space in your garden allows you to pack in more plants, and some plants require trellising to grow optimally. We use different trellising methods and materials depending on how much support a particular crop needs. For tomatoes, T-posts and twine offer an affordable, convenient option, but for plants with tendrils, like peas and cucumbers, you want more areas for the plants to grab. We use wire arches made from cattle panel, metal frames with jute twine woven in a lattice pattern, or a premade plastic trellis called a hortonova.

Trellising peppers

That last option is probably the easiest way to achieve a strong trellis quickly, but after cattle panels, it's the most expensive. In our backyard, we also make trellises for our pole beans using long, sturdy sticks in a tipi formation. You can make a trellis from found or reused materials in lots of different ways, so get creative!

T-POSTS: For trellising beans and tomatoes, creating tunnels, and erecting fences in our garden, we use metal T-posts. They are extremely strong and durable, and the notches make it easy to string up wire, twine, or other supports. If you're using a lot of them or have heavy or rocky soil, a metal T-post driver will save you a lot of time and energy in installing them. Just be sure to use proper ear protection!

In the Kitchen

DEHYDRATOR: In the kitchen, our number one preservation tool is the dehydrator. Ours runs basically 24/7 during the harvest season, and it allows us to store piles of dry vegetables, fruits, and mushrooms in our pantry at room temperature without the mess of canning or taking up limited freezer space. If you live in a particularly hot, dry climate, you can probably set an old screen outside in the sun, and it will have the same effect. Here in cloudy Pittsburgh, though, a dehydrator is a must-have.

GRAIN MILL: If you're growing any kind of grain, like flour corn, wheat, or oats, you'll want a good grain mill to grind it into grits, flour, and

meal. For years we used a coffee grinder to make cornmeal and masa. It worked, but it took *hours* to make a significant amount, and we had no control over the texture. A good hand-cranked grain mill gives you a ton of flexibility and efficiency. It's also a great arm workout!

STOCK POT: For water-bath canning, a big stock pot is essential. In that method, you boil the water and submerge your canned veggies in it for a set amount of time. Because some of the water cooks off, normal cooking pots sometimes don't hold enough water to cover the jars completely. In that case, you might risk a failed batch of canned veggies.

PRESSURE COOKER: In winter, a pressure cooker is great to have on hand for cooking staple crops, such as beans, flour corn, and pumpkin. We eat a lot of deer meat with our winter veggies, and our pressure cooker makes those big, hearty meals a breeze. Our model doesn't work for canning, but a traditional stovetop pressure cooker can pressure-can vegetables, which expands the horizons of what you can preserve in jars.

CANNING EQUIPMENT: If you plan on canning, obviously you need canning jars, lids, and rings. You can use the jars and rings over and over, but you shouldn't reuse the lids for canning. Every couple of years, we buy big boxes of canning lids to replenish our supply, but at this point we have enough jars that we only need to replace them if one breaks.

PLANT AND FUNGI BIOLOGY

As we brainstorm how to make likely the most boring chapter in this book more fun and engaging, we're coming up blank. If, when you read the word *biology,* your eyes glazed over and you want to skip this chapter for more fun information, do it with no shame. That said, the basic biology we cover here will help folks who might need a refresher. It also contains some fun nuggets for people like us who are fascinated by plants and fungi— which we have a sneaking suspicion you are!

Plant Biology 101

Depending on how you see the world, plants are magical alchemists or intricate factories— maybe both. They sprout from tiny seeds, grow roots deep into the earth, and generate energy to synthesize nutrients, vitamins, and phytochemicals out of thin air. And we mean that literally. Because plants absorb carbon dioxide from the air and use it to produce their carbon-based bodies through photosynthesis, they are literally building themselves from thin air. Plants are excellent at surviving, and our job as gardeners is to provide them with the conditions they need to thrive, then get out of the way. In exchange for us giving them a suitable place to grow, they give us the food we need to live.

COMMON PLANT TERMS

TRUE LEAVES VERSUS COTYLEDONS: Botanically speaking, there are two categories of leaves on each plant: the cotyledons and the true leaves. Cotyledons are simply the first leaf or leaves that emerge from a sprouted seed. They use the energy stored in the seed to work their way to the soil surface to reach sunlight and begin to generate energy through photosynthesis. After the cotyledons begin generating energy, the plant uses that energy to grow true leaves, which are essentially the adult version of the plant's leaves. Cotyledons are usually smaller and have more simple shapes than true leaves. Plants that initially sprout with one cotyledon are called monocots, and plants with two cotyledons are called dicots.

ROOTS AND TUBERS: Plant roots function like a combination of a drinking straw, stomach, and house foundation. They bury themselves deep in the soil to absorb water and nutrients, and they hold plants' sometimes gigantic bodies upright and tethered to the earth. Occasionally we also like to eat them. Carrots, beets, and sweet potatoes all have substantial, edible roots. Potatoes, often called "root crops," grow underground, but technically they're tubers, which store nutrients rather than absorbing them, as true roots do. Roots navigate through soil incredibly well, but compacted, hard soils can restrict them significantly. If your garden has particularly compacted soil, you'll notice that the roots grow only an inch or two into the ground before spreading sideways, which severely restricts the plant's ability to grow. In that case, breaking the soil with a broadfork or turning it over with a shovel and working in compost will create a much better environment for root growth.

PHOTOSYNTHESIS: The energy from every bite of food you've ever eaten—whether it came from a plant, an animal that ate plants, or a mushroom that grew on dead plants—came from nuclear fusion on the sun. Photosynthesis creates all food on earth. Photosynthesizing plants absorb energy from the sun, applying it to carbon dioxide and water, which react to produce oxygen and sugars in their leaves. They then use those sugars to grow roots, stems, leaves, and fruit. Most of the plants in this book need at least six hours of direct sunlight per day to produce enough energy to grow optimally. If they receive fewer than that, they will become malnourished because they can't produce enough sugar to grow properly.

VINES AND TENDRILS: When we think of vines, we often picture a plant wrapping around other plants or structures and climbing high to the sun. Most vines can support themselves by climbing structures, but some vining plants, like toma-

toes, vine but don't climb. They sprawl over the ground on flexible stems and need support from stakes and twine to grow vertically. Beans can climb other plants and structures by wrapping their stems around them as they grow. Other vining plants, such as peas, squash, and cucumbers, climb using tendrils. Tendrils are just modified stems or leaves that grab on to things to support a plant. They often appear as little springy coils and search for something to grab by growing in a circle. Once they hit something, their cells respond accordingly and the tendril grows to grab that support, whether a trellis, tree, or another stem. If you stood still next to a tendril long enough, it would eventually grab hold of you.

POLLINATION: Simply put, pollination means plant sex. Pollen grains containing microscopic sperm packets release from the "male" parts of flowers and transfer to the "female" parts, which contain eggs in ovules. When pollen lands on the female part of the flower, it sprouts a long tube into the flower that allows the sperm to travel and contact the egg. Plants have developed a lot of creative ways to transfer their pollen. All the crops in this book are self-pollinated, insect-pollinated, or wind-pollinated.

Self-pollinated plants have male and female parts on the same flowers, and pollination takes place when some of the pollen from the male part matures and falls onto the female part. With these plants, such as beans and peppers, very little genetic transfer happens because the pollen stays within one individual.

For some plants, like squash, cucumbers, and melons, insects carry pollen from the male part to the female part. Often these plants have separate male and female flowers, and the pollen arrives on the female flower by sticking to the legs or body of a hungry insect. In exchange for

the pollen transfer, the flowers feed the insects sugary nectar and protein-rich pollen.

Wind-pollinated plants have tiny pollen grains that are light enough to float on the wind. The pollen blows from the male part and finds the female part on a wing and a prayer. These plants, such as corn, often produce a *ton* of pollen to ensure that some of it makes it to the female part of the plant.

FRUIT VERSUS VEGETABLE: Many pointless dinner table arguments have been had over the difference between a fruit and a vegetable, but botanically speaking, fruits and veggies have clear distinctions. A fruit is the ripe ovary of a flowering plant. A fleshy material surrounds the seeds to protect them and provide possible nutrition once they sprout or to make the whole package an attractive snack for animals who might disperse those seeds to new locations. Over the centuries, we've selected the fruits we grow in our gardens to function as much more than seed-dispersal devices, prizing them for their sweetness, size, or ability to store well.

Technically, a lot of what we consider vegetables qualify as fruits because they meet this definition: tomatoes, squash, peppers, cucumbers, corn, and beans.

A vegetable refers to the vegetative parts of a plant that we eat, such as stalks, leaves, flowers, and roots. Colloquially, though, we all pretty much call the sweet ones "fruit" and the savory ones "vegetables," which is mostly how we refer to produce in this book.

Fungi Biology 101

Because they often grow from the ground or on plants and don't move like animals, we tend to think of fungi as another type of plant. In a lot of ways, though, fungi resemble animals more than plants. Like animals, fungi can't produce their own food. They need to consume plants or animals for energy. You might be having a hard time imagining how something without a mouth could "consume" a plant or animal. Fungi "stomachs" exist on the outside of their bodies, or rather their stomachs kind of *are* their bodies. The white mycelium of wood-rotting fungi, such

A mushroom spore print

as shiitake and oyster mushrooms, grows into plant material and secretes enzymes that digest that material from the inside out. As the plants break down, the mycelium absorbs the nutrients and uses them to grow and produce the mushrooms we eat.

COMMON FUNGI TERMS

SPORES: Every day, each mature mushroom produces billions of spores, essentially the seeds of fungi, and they float on the wind in search of a new place to grow. If they land on a suitable host, they can grow into a new organism and eventually produce their own spores. Each individual spore is microscopic, but you can see them en masse by placing a mushroom cap, gill side down, on a sheet of paper, where the spores will leave a beautiful pattern. Spores have variable colors from species to species, so they can be a helpful feature for confidently identifying wild mushrooms.

MYCELIUM: This part of the fungus functions as its body: arms for grabbing, legs for traveling, stomach for digesting, and maybe even the brain. Often you can see it with the naked eye. If you've left food in the refrigerator for too long and later found it covered with a white, fuzzy mass, that's the mycelium of mold, which is a type of fungus. When growing oyster mushrooms, you can watch the mycelium expand and consume the growing material, the grow bag slowly turning into a white mass, day after day.

MUSHROOMS: People sometimes use the words *mushroom* and *fungus* interchangeably. All mushrooms are fungi, but not all fungi produce mushrooms. Some fungi use mushrooms to produce spores and spread their offspring. They're not "fruit" in the botanical sense, but we often refer to them as the "fruit" or "fruiting bodies" of fungi. For shiitakes and oyster mushrooms, the fungi in this book, we harvest and consume the mushroom.

See, that was kind of fun to read, right? We knew you were a biology nerd!

GARDEN PLANNING

On a cold evening, curling up on the couch with a stack of seed catalogs, circling whatever catches our eye with a fat marker, is an excellent remedy for the winter blues. In those moments, with no pests or weeds in sight, no blazing heat or unseasonable drought, growing anything seems possible and the space in our garden feels infinite. Good garden planning means balancing that feeling of limitless potential with the physical constraints of your space and climate. It's a time to dream big while also paying attention to the details.

Some gardeners prefer to wing it, sowing seeds in warm soil and bedding plants on a whim. That approach can be fun, and we certainly encourage creativity and experimentation in the garden, but if you want to grow a lot of food efficiently, a good plan for what to plant when and where is essential. Here's our best advice for making a solid, organized garden plan.

Mapping Your Garden

Planning your garden will go much easier if you can visualize the growing space, so we recommend drawing a map of your garden. It doesn't have to look like a work of art, but it should adhere to scale, showing the square feet or meters you have per bed and how your garden orients to the cardinal directions. It also can help to include other information that will affect growing decisions, such as a big tree that shades part of a bed or a steep slope that makes one side of the garden harder to access. When deciding what to grow, first plan around these physical barriers. Under the tree, for example, you could plan to grow leafy greens that don't mind a bit of shade, such as kale and spinach, and in steep areas stick to sprawling crops that only need to be harvested once, such as winter squash and pumpkins.

We like to list what we want to grow in descending order, from what we want the most to what we need only a little bit. If you're aiming for a balanced garden diet, dedicate a large proportion of your space to starchy and protein-rich staples, like corn and legumes. (See the Living off Your Garden chapter, page xvii, for more.) But plan your garden around what *you* will eat most often. If you love tomatoes and want to eat them by the bowlful year-round, put them at the top of your list! If you want enough kale for a few salads but hate cooked kale, slot that one at the bottom.

PLANT SPACING

Different plants have vastly different space requirements. Especially for new gardeners, it can feel tempting to cram as many crops as possible into a bed, but we urge you not to do this. Overcrowded plants have to compete for water, sunlight, and nutrients. Plants competing for nutrients usually end up stunted or weak, which may make them more susceptible to pests and disease. Seed packets usually give recommended plant spacing, but the "row spacing" on many packets often refers to large-scale growing using a tractor to cultivate between rows—usually irrelevant to home gardeners!

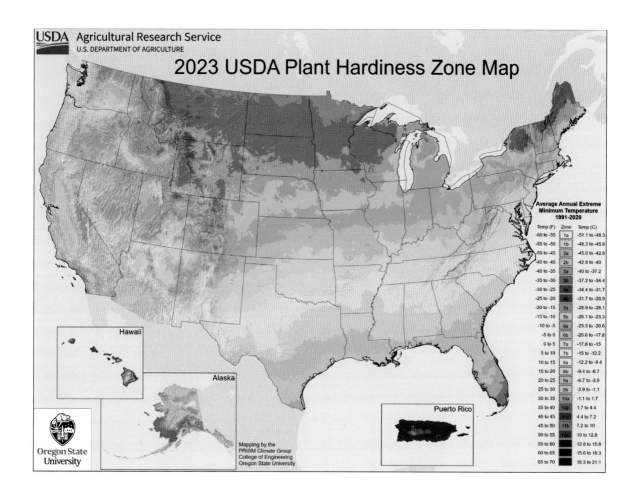

2023 USDA Plant Hardiness Zone Map

USDA Agricultural Research Service
U.S. DEPARTMENT OF AGRICULTURE

Check the guidelines in our crop chapters for our recommended spacing.

Use your garden map and those guidelines to assign spaces to your future plants. We like to start with top-priority plants, keeping in mind how many plants total we want to grow for the year and starting with those that take up the most space, including corn, potatoes, tomatoes, and squash.

Seasonality

GROWING ZONE

Most gardening books and videos mention "growing zones," "hardiness zones," or just "zones" a lot. The term refers to the segmented map of annual average minimum temperatures.

We've included a map for the United States, which was the only one we could find publicly available to print. If you live outside the United States, search online for your country's name and "growing zones." Hardiness zones help show which plants will grow well in your area and which won't. This information is especially important for perennial plants, like fruit trees, but it's also critical for an annual vegetable garden because of the first and last frost dates.

First and Last Frost

In temperate climates, each growing zone has an average first frost date in the fall when you can expect the temperature to drop below 32°F, which will kill many warm-season vegetables. This date typically marks the end of the growing season and beginning of winter. As spring comes, your growing zone also will have an average last frost date: the last day in the season that you can expect the temperature to fall below freezing. We'll get into more detail in the specific crop chapters, but these dates can play an important role in helping you plan your garden. Use the zone maps to find your zone, then look up your zone's first and last frost dates.

When mapping your garden, keep in mind when the plants grow best throughout the year. Warm-weather crops, like tomatoes and beans, will die if exposed to freezing temperatures, whereas other plants prefer or even require cold temperatures. Spinach, radishes, and arugula thrive in cooler weather. They usually won't die if exposed to hot, sunny days, but they may go to seed before fully mature and ready to harvest. On your garden map, indicate when you'll plant specific crops outside. You can't plant warm-season crops outdoors until after the last frost in your area, so you can grow cool-season crops in that space as long as you harvest them in time for you to plant the summer crops.

SUCCESSION PLANTING

Depending on the growing zone, most of the crops in this book don't take a full season to produce. If you just grow one crop in each bed, that bed will be unproductive at some point in the season. To maximize output, plan to grow multiple crops in succession in each area. This strategy works well with crops that grow in different seasons, such as growing radishes in early spring, harvesting them, and then planting green beans for summer. If you want to have a lot of a particular vegetable throughout the growing season, keep a space free for succession planting and stagger your planting times accordingly. Planting a small section of fast-growing greens every two weeks can keep a family in salad all year long.

Most seed packets include "days to maturity" information. If not, search the variety name plus "days to maturity." This number tells you the average number of days for that variety, whether leafy greens or squash, to begin producing fruits or vegetables. This information will help you plan your garden successions because you can estimate when crops will come out based on when you put them in. You also can determine whether you have enough time to put in a particular variety based on last and first frost dates. Keep in mind that these are just averages, and it may take less time or more depending on your climate and growing conditions. It's wise to add extra time for growth delays and transition time between crops.

> **Successions that work well for us:**
>
> - Green beans after garlic in summer
> - Peas before or after summer squash
> - Fall kale or collards after summer squash
> - Overwintered onions before tomatoes or peppers

COMPANION PLANTING

Like us, you probably don't have unlimited space to grow your food. So you'll have to be smart about what you plant to maximize your harvest. Companion planting provides one of the best ways to do this. You can grow corn in one bed, beans in another, and squash in a third, or you could grow all three in the same bed in a traditional Three Sisters garden and use the other two beds for different crops.

Even if you're not growing plants that support one another, think about optimizing spacing when planning your garden. Vining plants, like squash, can grow on the edges of beds to spill onto pathways or down hills, leaving the more valuable real estate to the crops that need it most, like root vegetables. Vining crops can grow up a trellis, making them easy to harvest and providing shade for a more sensitive plant below, such as cilantro or lettuce. Fast-growing vegetables, including radishes and lettuce, can go between crops that mature more slowly, such as tomatoes, kale, and collards, since you'll harvest them before the canopies of the slower growing crops fill and block their sunlight.

If you're starting your first garden, we recommend beginning with just a few crops that you want to master before trying to cram in every vegetable or fruit your grocery store sells. When you start growing your food, it's easy to feel overwhelmed with all the crops you can grow. Trying to learn the details and needs of every one of them in a single season is a great recipe for stress and burnout. (Ask us how we know.) Take a look at that list of crops you most want to eat and begin with those. Each year, as you gain confidence, you can add more crops and varieties. Before you know it, you'll be harvesting wide-ranging feasts from your dream garden. That's the great thing about gardening, after all. There's always next year!

BED PREP

If you're a new gardener and just selected your garden space or built your raised beds, you need to prepare the soil for the growing season. The same point holds true for gardeners with an established garden, but that case starts a few steps ahead. How you prepare your beds for planting depends heavily on the state of your soil. Various bed-preparation methods have their benefits and drawbacks. We'll explain our preferred methods and why we like them, but experiment a little and figure out what works best for your garden.

Fertilization

Proper fertilization can often make the difference between a lush, thriving garden and an anemic, struggling patch of dirt. If you send a soil sample for analysis as we discuss in the Soil Fertility and Nutrient Cycles chapter (page 23), you can add amendments to increase whichever elements fell below ideal levels in your soil. Testing your soil isn't totally necessary, but it can help you avoid wasting money on fertilizer for nutrients that your garden might already have in abundance.

Good-quality compost, homemade or bought, will provide some nutrients as well as lots of organic matter, which is essential for feeding beneficial soil microorganisms. Every year, usually right before seeding or transplanting in spring, we add about 1 inch of homemade compost to our beds. If you don't have a good way to access compost, don't fret. You can add organic matter and carbon to your soil in other ways, such as mulching or growing cover crops.

We recommend fertilizing with feather meal for nitrogen deficiencies, bone meal for phosphorus deficiencies, and compost for potassium deficiencies.

Cover Crops

In addition to keeping garden beds weed-free in the offseason, cover crops are an excellent way to add fertility and organic matter to your beds. We use cover crops heavily in spring before planting our main crops.

Our favorite cover crop method is planting legumes, like peas and clover, in early spring, then weed-whacking them down before planting corn, beans, and squash. The decaying legume plants

A cover crop of clover

release carbon and nitrogen into the soil, the leaves and stems form a mulch that helps retain water and deter weeds, and the roots support healthy soil organisms and add organic matter.

Between spring and fall crops, you can plant a cover crop, such as buckwheat, to keep the soil covered and retain nutrients. Last year, after harvesting our spring radishes and spinach, we grew buckwheat in our raised beds over the summer. Then, in late summer, we whacked it down and planted cabbages directly in the buckwheat mulch.

In the late fall, we like to sow winter rye in all the beds not growing anything over the winter. Winter rye is an extremely cold-hardy cereal crop that establishes quickly, so you can sow it much later in the year than other cover crops. If you grow crops that come out earlier in the year, such as a flour corn that is done in early fall, you can add other plants to your cover crop mix, creating even more biomass and root structure to build your soil. A mixture of clover, rye, and daikon radishes provides multiple benefits for the soil.

Tilling

No matter how much fertility your soil has, vegetable crops won't grow in it if the soil is too compacted for their roots to expand or access water and oxygen. Compacted soil feels rock-hard when you try to dig in with a spade. If that's the case, you likely need to till it and work in organic matter at least once.

Because tilling disrupts the soil structure and reduces populations of beneficial soil organisms, we recommend doing it only once to break up the soil, then converting to a no-till system. That said, every garden is different. If you have particularly heavy clay soil, it may help to grow and till in a few rounds of cover crops to add organic matter to the native soil over a couple of seasons.

Tilling mixes the top several inches of soil, including all the weeds or other plants growing in it. It's a quick and convenient way to prepare soil for seeding. However, that soil disturbance also brings buried weed seeds closer to the surface, where they receive the conditions necessary to germinate and grow. Tilled garden beds require consistent weeding throughout the season.

No-Till

No-till growing is exactly what it sounds like. You can use this method in a number of ways, but the main principle is to avoid disturbing the soil as much as possible. Keeping soil structure intact protects the beneficial insects, fungi, bacteria, and other organisms that add fertility, retain moisture, and prevent erosion. Weed seeds also stay deep in the soil, where they can't germinate, so the weeds in your garden will come only from seeds that blow onto your soil during the growing season—or from perennial weeds that you can pull by hand to reduce their population over time.

To prepare for planting, you can put a thick layer of compost on your bed to smother small weeds and create a loose medium in which seeds and plant roots can grow. Many gardeners put cardboard down first to provide an additional barrier against grass or weeds. In the moist environment, the cardboard breaks down quickly, allowing the crop roots to grow through it. We prefer this bed-preparation method, but it requires a lot of compost, which can be expensive for large gardens.

SEED SOURCING

A lot of confusing information about seeds floats through the gardening world, much of it related to genetically modified organism (GMO) seeds. GMO seeds are seeds that are modified using gene-splicing technology to insert traits from other plants or organisms as a shortcut around traditional plant breeding. New gardeners often ask us where to find non-GMO seeds because they heard somewhere that all seeds are GMO now. As gardeners and farmers with more than two decades of experience between us, neither of us has ever come across a GMO seed. GMO seeds are primarily sold commercially to massive farms, and for the most part they are limited to staple crops like feed corn and soybeans. As we write this book, the only GMO seed on the retail market for gardeners is a tomato with snapdragon DNA that contains a lot of the antioxidant anthocyanin. Under the current USDA organic standards, no GMO crops can be grown on organic farms. If that's something you're trying to avoid, buying certified USDA organic seeds guarantees that they are not genetically modified. Now that that big question is out of the way, let's talk about sourcing seeds!

Lots of excellent retailers specialize in heirloom varieties of vegetables and fruits geared specifically toward gardeners and small farmers. When we were running our small farm and regularly ordering a large number of vegetable seeds in bulk, our go-to was often High Mowing Organic Seeds. All of their seeds are USDA certified organic, and we have never had an issue with germination rates or an incorrect order. High Mowing carries a few unique heirloom varieties, but they primarily focus on crops that produce consistently for small market farmers.

For heirloom beans, corn, and squash, we go to the folks who developed and stewarded those crops for thousands of years and order from the Alliance of Native Seedkeepers. This company was started by a group of Indigenous American seedkeepers with a mission to maintain their cultural foodways. They provide gardeners and farmers with incredible varieties of American heirlooms that have been grown here for generations, and they aim to rebuild the spiritual bond many Indigenous people share with these crops.

For staple grains, like flour, corn, oats, wheat, and rice, Fedco Seeds is an excellent option. Fedco Seeds is a worker-owned cooperative that aims to support small and independent growers. They carry many wonderful heirloom vegetables, including some unique varieties of important staple crops.

Truelove Seeds is our favorite source for some of the seeds that are culturally important to us. They maintain important varieties, like koosa, Aleppo pepper, and chickpeas. Part of their mission is to provide a source of seeds from home to different diaspora communities living in America. Among these are their African diaspora seeds; East Asian seeds; Italian seeds; and Seeds

of the Levant, which includes some of the Syrian, Palestinian and Lebanese varieties so important to Jordan's family.

In the Seed Saving chapter (page 51), we'll discuss how to save your own seeds to preserve and improve your crops, but to do that, you want to start with seeds labeled "heirloom" or "open-pollinated." Heirloom or open-pollinated seeds have been traditionally bred and retain their characteristics from one season to the next. The alternative, called hybrid or F1 seeds, are often made by cross-pollinating open-pollinated varieties. Hybrid seeds can provide wonderful vegetables, but if you save seeds from them, the crops those seeds produce are often very different from the original hybrid. Seed packets or web-site descriptions categorize all seeds as open-pollinated/heirloom or hybrid/F1.

Each winter, many heirloom seed companies mail catalogs that showcase their best varieties. As we mentioned at the start of the Garden Planning chapter, one of our favorite winter activities is flipping through seed catalogs, looking for new varieties to grow in the coming season. This activity is about 10 percent garden planning and 90 percent daydreaming about the spring. We also love discovering new seeds through seed swaps with other gardeners and friends. Our city actually has a massive seed swap at a library every year, and we've found some great varieties that way. Seed swaps provide a great opportunity to talk with somebody who has grown the exact variety of fruit or vegetable in your area so you'll know what to expect.

SEED STARTING

Before we dive into the subject of seed starting, we want to make it clear that there's absolutely nothing wrong with buying seedlings from a garden center. If you're a new gardener, you have a lot to learn in your first year, and starting each crop from seed can be a daunting task. Fruit and vegetable seedlings are widely available at garden centers, so don't feel any shame if you opt to skip this step for now. That said, garden centers typically offer only a tiny fraction of the existing crop varieties, and in the case of big-box stores, they are often not varieties that were bred to grow optimally in your area.

Learning to start your own seedlings allows you to select specific varieties from seed catalogs and trade local seeds with other gardeners. So when you're planning your garden, you can choose from *hundreds* of unique tomato varieties rather than the two or three your garden center might have. Once you know how to start your own seeds, you can also grow plants from seeds you've saved from the previous season. From there, you can begin to develop your own variet-ies bred for your specific garden climate, as we discuss in the Seed Saving chapter (page 51).

While starting your garden from seed *is* considered an advanced gardening task, there's really not much to it. Seeds have one mission: to sprout and grow into a plant. They wait for the opportune combination of moisture, warmth, and light before cracking open and emerging from the safety of their shells. Once they emerge, the tender seedlings are fragile and require

specific conditions to survive and thrive. Creating those optimal conditions at home is simple but requires a little bit of equipment and seed-starting know-how.

Equipment

Starting seeds at home requires four basic elements: a container, potting soil, seeds, and moisture. Your container can be anything from a purpose-built seedling tray to an egg carton with holes punched in the bottom. You can buy potting soil from any garden center or you can use homemade compost, but compost is a bit more likely to cause mold issues on your seedlings. Fresh out of the bag, potting soil tends to be hydrophobic (from the Greek for "fear of water"), so thoroughly moisten it before filling the container; otherwise, the water just runs right through it. We load our potting soil into a 5-gallon bucket and add water until it holds together when squeezed but isn't dripping. After you initially hydrate the potting soil, it will stay moist as long as you regularly wet it with a spray bottle or watering can.

Light

All seedlings need access to ample sunlight or full-spectrum grow lights to avoid becoming "leggy." This term describes plants that are lacking sunlight and, in a last-ditch effort to access it, they focus all their energy on growing tall and lanky to try to reach some light. We think it's actually kind of sad. This results in seedlings with stunted root systems that struggle to hold the plant up and they often never fully recover, even when transplanted into a garden with plenty of sunlight.

For a strong start in life, your seedlings need around 12 hours of light per day. Often gardeners are starting seedlings indoors in winter or early spring, when the sun is low in the sky, so a sunny window won't suffice unless you supplement it with a grow light. Full-spectrum LED grow lights are widely available online, and they get more affordable every year. If you are starting summer crops when the weather is warm, you can set up your seed-starting station in a sunny spot outside. When your seedlings emerge, keep a close eye on them for the first few days—they'll tell you what they need. If they look leggy or pale, increase their sunlight exposure by moving them to a sunnier location or moving your grow lights closer to the plants to increase their exposure. When our seedlings first emerge, we hang our grow lights about 3 inches above the seedling tray to maximize their exposure.

Water

From the moment you place your seeds in potting soil, you never want the soil to dry out completely. It's healthy for the surface of the soil to dry out once per day, and you don't want the seedlings themselves to be constantly dripping with water, but you never want the potting soil to dry all the way through. The best test for dryness is to pick up the corner of your trays or containers and feel the weight. If it feels unusually light, it's probably dry and likely needs more frequent watering. If it feels substantial and heavy, you are likely watering adequately.

If your plants are constantly dripping wet, they are at risk of developing a fungal disease referred to as "damping off." If this takes hold and your plants start falling over and rotting, you'll need to start the seedlings over and reduce your watering frequency. One effective way to prevent fungal diseases on your seedlings is to increase the airflow in your seed-starting station by setting up a fan to lightly blow air over the seedlings. The movement from this airflow will also help your seedlings develop strong stems.

Hardening Off

Deciding when your seedlings are ready to graduate and face the real world in the garden is partly personal preference, but we'll cover some general rules of thumb for each crop in the specific crop chapters. Regardless of when you choose to kick them out of the nest, make sure they are acclimated to the outside weather before transplanting them into the garden.

The coddled conditions of your seed station—consistent light, moisture, and temperature—have made your seedlings healthy but soft. They need to toughen up a bit before heading into the harsh conditions outside. To acclimate them to outdoor conditions, a process called "hardening off," carry your seedlings outside during the day to experience some mild outdoor conditions, then bring them back in at night. Repeat this process for three to five days. After that, your seedlings can handle whatever the garden throws at them.

This is probably obvious, but hardening off is only necessary if you're starting your seeds indoors in the early spring. If you're starting summer seedlings in trays outdoors or you're direct-seeding crops in the garden, they will naturally acclimate to the conditions as they develop.

Transplanting

After you've hardened off seedlings to move to their forever home in the garden, most of the hard work has taken place already, and it's time to let the plants work their magic. Spacing and planting depth vary for each crop, as detailed in the specific crop chapters, but all seedlings need heavy watering before being transplanted into the soil. Experienced gardeners often say, "You need to soak them to the bone." This initial watering gets them off to a strong start and helps loosen roots that may have tangled slightly in the seedling containers.

After soaking the container, remove each seedling by squeezing the cell and turning the whole tray or pot sideways so the plant slides out on its own. This method avoids breaking the roots or stems, as can happen if you just pull the plant from the cell.

When you remove the seedling from its cell, inspect the root ball to ensure it's not overgrown. If you find a mass of roots tangled around one another that holds the exact shape of the container, you may have let your seedlings grow a little too long. Seedlings with root balls like this are called "root-bound." If you plant root-bound seedlings, the roots will continue growing in circles and never develop a healthy foundation. To mitigate this issue, soak root-bound seedlings for a few minutes and gently work the roots with your fingers to untangle them before planting. Take care to untangle them without breaking too many of the roots. It's fine if you rip a few, but you want as many as possible to stay intact.

Once your seedlings have gone into the ground, water the area around them well and make sure it stays consistently watered through rain or irrigation for at least a week, which will give the plant time to establish itself and develop deep roots. From here, your plants are well on their way to providing you with a bounty of fresh veggies and fruit!

SOIL FERTILITY AND NUTRIENT CYCLES

Growing food can feel like magic. Pop a little seed in the ground, and it bursts through the soil surface and morphs into a plant, seemingly from thin air. It uses energy generated from a distant, flaming ball of plasma to photosynthesize and produce carbohydrates, proteins, and fats that we eat to fuel our bodies. Because plants nourish themselves so differently than we do, it's easy to forget that they need to eat as well! Plants produce their own energy from sunlight, but they also need micronutrients. You could eat a stick of butter every day and have plenty of calories to stay alive, but you need protein, vitamins, and minerals to stay healthy.

Nitrogen (N), phosphorus (P), and potassium (K) make or break the health of the plants in our gardens. Plants use tons of other elements to grow, but those three, commonly abbreviated as NPK, occur naturally in soil the least, making them most likely to limit plant growth. A deficiency in any one of those three elements can result in stunted plants, low fruit production, and susceptibility to pests and diseases.

In wild ecosystems, these nutrients are cycled from place to place through animals' urine, feces, and eventually their bodily decay. They are also passed around by the decomposition of dead plant material and through massive networks of fungi under the soil that scientists are only recently beginning to study. Nutrient cycles in wild ecosystems are a little different from the nutrient cycles of many industrial farms and conventional gardens because they're just that: a cycle.

Imagine following a single nitrogen molecule around a forest. One spring afternoon, nitrogen-fixing bacteria in the soil snatch it from the air and convert it to a form that can be used to fuel

plant growth. The bacteria trades the nitrogen to a plant in exchange for shelter in the plant's root nodules. The plant uses that nitrogen to create proteins and leafy growth. The nitrogen spends the spring tangled in the proteins of a tender green leaf until a white-tailed deer eats the leaf

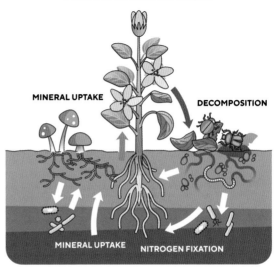

SOIL FOOD WEB AND NUTRIENT CYCLING

MINERAL UPTAKE

DECOMPOSITION

MINERAL UPTAKE   NITROGEN FIXATION

in the morning sun. The deer digests the leaf, and the nitrogen releases back into its elemental form in her gut. The next day, it is returned to the soil along with a host of other nutrients in the deer's urine. The urine is absorbed by the soil where the nitrogen can once again be taken up by a plant, used to grow leaves and fruit, eaten again and so on and so on.

Now let's follow a nitrogen molecule through a typical industrial farm. Early in the spring, the molecule is sucked out of the air and into a factory furnace, where it is brought to extremely hot temperatures and combined with hydrogen gas and iron to convert it into a form that can be used by plants. The nitrogen gas is condensed and pumped into a tanker that ships it across the globe. The tanker is unloaded onto a truck, driven hundreds of miles down a highway, and delivered to a massive farm. The condensed nitrogen is pumped into a tractor tank, then sprayed over vast acres of newly emerging cabbage. The cabbage roots quickly absorb the nitrogen, using it to produce thick green leaves. It sits in those leaves all spring until the cabbage is harvested, thrown into a crate, and shipped across the country to a grocery store. A human buys the cabbage, drives it home, transforms it into a delicious meal, and digests it. The nitrogen is released from the cabbage leaf in the human's gut, and the next morning it is flushed down the toilet. The human waste runs through pipes beneath the city streets and into a sewage-treatment plant to be sterilized and pumped into a river, where it flows into the ocean, never to see farmland again.

Since the conception of agriculture roughly 10,000 years ago, people growing food have fertilized their soil using sustainable practices that mimic the more natural nutrient cycle. Practices like growing nitrogen-fixing cover crops, grazing animals through the fields, and planting companion plants were commonplace. It wasn't until

Combine harvester on conventional farm

the early 1900s that commercial farmers began injecting their fields with synthetic fertilizers to boost crop growth. This "miracle of modern technology" meant that farmers no longer had to worry about maintaining the nutrient cycle in their fields because they could pump their soil full of factory-made liquid fertilizer and the crops would grow just fine. Synthetic fertilizers gave rise to affordable, industrially produced food as people left rural, agrarian areas for cities. Thankfully this likely helped us avoid a global famine at the turn of the 20th century, but it was not without ecological consequences.

Farms that regularly apply synthetic fertilizer and ignore soil health often have dry, cracking soil devoid of the vast networks of fungi, bacteria, and invertebrates that maintain healthy soils. Because the soil on these farms is more or less devoid of life, there is little to tie it together and hold nutrients in place. The 1930s agricultural catastrophe that we refer to as the Dust Bowl in the United States—where large swaths of commercial farmland essentially just blew away in the wind—was partially brought on by industrial farms transforming the lush American prairie into a barren, dusty wasteland. Unfortunately, this type of farm leaches more than just soil. Every year, rainfall washes *tons* of excess commercial fertilizer and soil into streams and rivers. It accumulates and runs into ponds, lakes, and oceans. The massive influx of elements like nitrogen and phosphorus into waterways leads to explosions of algae growth that throw off the balance of the ecosystem and cause massive dead zones, where no aquatic life can survive until the nutrients are allowed to rebalance.[4]

Alternatively, healthy garden soils are bustling with colonies of beneficial bacteria and fungi, packed with organic matter (broken-down plants), and wriggling with invertebrates that transport nutrients and aerate the soil. This thriving subterranean ecosystem ties healthy soils together, making them less susceptible to erosion, allowing them to hold on to more rainwater, and reducing the amount of nutrients they leach into the environment. Maintaining soil health not only benefits our environment, but it also makes growing food more hands-off by allowing us to water less, apply fewer fertilizer inputs, and grow more productive, nutrient-dense crops.

Home gardeners don't need to be chemistry experts to grow healthy crops, but it is important for us to understand those three critical elements, NPK, to keep our crops as healthy as possible.

Nitrogen (N)

Take a breath of air and hold it in while you read the next sentence. The air that you are currently holding in your lungs is about 78 percent nitrogen gas. OK, exhale. How could nitrogen possibly be limiting plant growth if it's literally making up most of the air we breathe? To put it simply, the nitrogen floating in our air is in a form that

Legume root nodules

---

4 https://www.epa.gov/nutrientpollution/effects-dead-zones-and-harmful-algal-blooms

plants can't absorb or use for their growth. Luckily, the bacteria in the soil that we discussed in the forest nutrient cycle have the amazing ability to capture that nitrogen gas from the air and convert it to a form that plants can absorb and use. These nitrogen-fixing bacteria trade the bioactive nitrogen to certain plants through their roots in exchange for shelter in the form of small bumps called root nodules. You can actually see these bacteria hotels with the naked eye on the roots of crops like beans and peas.

Nitrogen is very important to animals when it comes to forming proteins, but a lot of it passes right through us as we digest our food. That's why animal manure and urine are considered among the best sources of natural nitrogen fertilizer. Chicken and cow manure is actually so rich in nitrogen that it can overwhelm and even kill plants if it is applied directly to them without first being composted or diluted. If you have a yard and a dog, you might be familiar with this phenomenon, called "burning." The yellow patches of grass left behind where they pee and poop are essentially from the grass overdosing on nitrogen fertilizer.

In our gardens, we primarily go straight to the source for much of our nitrogen fertilizer, using plants that host nitrogen-fixing bacteria in their roots to pull it from the air. In early spring, we plant hardy winter peas inoculated with nitrogen-fixing bacteria and allow them to grow until they create a nice patch of nitrogen-rich biomass. The peas take up that nitrogen and use it to grow roots, stems, and leaves. Eventually, we mow or weed-whack the peas, killing the plants and turning all their leaves, stems, and roots into a dense mulch. We plant our crops in that nitrogen-filled biomass, which slowly fuels their growth as it decomposes and the nitrogen releases back into the soil. We also supplement the plant-derived nitrogen with animal sources, including feather meal, composted chicken manure, and fish emulsion for heavy nitrogen feeders, such as flour corn.

Phosphorus (P)

In 1669, German alchemist Hennig Brand was attempting to synthesize gold from human urine . . . interesting times! He collected gallons of urine from his beer-drinking neighbors, fermented it, and cooked away the liquid until all that was left was a waxy white substance that easily ignited into a bright flame. Unbeknownst to him at the time, what he had actually discovered was something much more precious than gold: pure phosphorus. Despite Brand's discovery, we haven't yet turned to human urine as a major source of phosphorus fertilizer. In modern commercial agriculture, phosphorus fertilizer primarily comes from finite sources of mined rock phosphate.

The massive mining operations that extract rock phosphate use some of the largest machines on earth to dig and transport truckloads of fertilizer, exporting it to farms all over the planet. Much of this fertilizer is applied to farms with dead, eroding soil, then lost to runoff. At current consumption levels, the US Geological Survey estimates that we have just a few hundred years of global rock phosphate reserves left. In the unlikely case that you're reading this book in the year 2225, we sincerely hope that humans have changed our behavior and a more sustainable phosphorus cycle fertilized your food. Otherwise, well . . . good luck!

Because animals excrete nearly all the phosphorus that we consume, animal waste is an excellent renewable source of the element. Islands full of seabird guano are so rich in phosphorus that wars have been fought over them.

The United States actually passed a law in 1856, the Guano Islands Act, that allowed any citizen to take possession of any "uninhabited island" containing guano in the name of the United States. We shudder at the thought of their definition of "uninhabited island" in the 1850s. While we don't recommend colonizing islands containing guano, composted livestock manure and urine are excellent renewable sources of phosphorus.

Animal bones also contain tons of phosphate and calcium, so bone meal from farm-raised or hunted animals makes a great, slow-release phosphorus and calcium fertilizer.

During hunting season, after extracting the last food value from the bones of fish and deer, we dehydrate them in the sun or oven, then pulverize them into bone meal. If that's a little more than you want to do, you can buy bags of bone meal at most garden centers.

Potassium (K)

The fancy, scientific-sounding word *potassium* comes from the phrase "pot ash," which is what preindustrial English farmers called the fertilizer they produced by burning wood and leaves in a pot. By weight, wood ashes contain about 10 percent potassium and 25 percent calcium carbonate, making wood ash a great source of potassium. Calcium carbonate raises the pH of the soil, however, which can be problematic if you already have alkaline soil, meaning it has a pH above 7. (Fun fact: The root of the word *alkaline* derives from the ancient Arabic *al qalyah*, which *also* means "plant ashes." Aren't words fun?)

Similar to phosphorus, most potassium fertilizer used on commercial farms is mined from nonrenewable mineral sources. Also similar to phosphorus, much of the potassium fertilizer applied to these vast commercial fields is lost to erosion and runoff, meaning growers need to truck it in and reapply it in great amounts every season.

Composted plant material provides an excellent source of potassium. At the end of each growing season, small-scale growers like you and us can recycle the nutrient over and over by breaking down spent plants and food scraps and returning them to garden beds in the form of rich compost. You can replace the small percentage of potassium pulled from your garden's nutrient cycle and flushed down the toilet by using composted animal manure, kelp meal, or other organic fertilizers.

Soil Testing

Try not to feel overwhelmed by all this soil chemistry or knowing the levels of every single compound or element in your soil. Humans successfully grew food for thousands of years without knowing about these substances. The best test for soil health is how your plants are growing. If they're growing well, chances are your soil has a good balance of the necessary nutrients and minerals. You can keep it in good shape with cover cropping and annual additions of compost and a balanced organic fertilizer. But if some of your plants are struggling to grow or constantly beset by developmental problems like blossom-end rot or disease, it might be time for a soil test.

As we mentioned in the Site Selection chapter (page 3), it's always a good idea to test your soil for heavy-metal contamination if you live in an urban area or are starting your garden on a site where an old building once stood. But you can test your soil for its nutrient profile, too. The easiest way to do this is to take a soil sample in the fall or early spring and send it to a soil lab. Agricultural universities throughout North America and elsewhere offer affordable mail-in soil testing.

To take a soil sample, dig down 6 to 8 inches into your garden bed or future garden area. If you're managing areas in your garden differently or already see notable differences in soil quality or how plants grow in them, keep the samples separate, so you can test them independently. Likewise, if you have concerns about contamination in one spot but not in others, keep those samples separate. Our house is almost 100 years old, so we knew the surrounding ground had the potential for lead contamination from paint or other materials. When we started our garden, we separately tested a large bed that we made next to the house. Luckily, it turned out to be safe to grow in.

For each sample, most soil labs require 1 to 2 cups of soil. Within each area, take several samples at random and mix them to determine an average across that space. Let them dry at room temperature until crumbly, then seal them in a clean container, such as a sealable plastic bag. Label your samples clearly so you remember where they came from in your garden. The lab will have specific instructions on how to mail your samples.

OK, now that we've talked through nutrient cycles and maintaining healthy soils, let's follow one more nitrogen molecule, this time through a sustainable vegetable garden.

In early spring, nitrogen-fixing bacteria in the soil pull the molecule from the air and trade it to a winter pea plant in exchange for shelter in its roots. The plant draws the nitrogen into its leaves, where it sits until an electric weed-whacker chops down the plant. As the leaf decomposes, the nitrogen releases into the soil, where the roots of a flour cornstalk absorb it. The corn uses the molecule to produce protein in its substantial blue kernels. After the kernels mature and dry, the gardener picks the ear by hand, grinds it into cornmeal, and cooks it into beautiful blue-green corn bread. The gardener digests the corn bread and, the next day, pees on their compost pile. The pile of rich organic matter absorbs the nitrogen, and the urine is sterilized over the winter by ammonia, soil microorganisms, and heat. The next spring, that nutrient-rich compost is spread onto fresh garden beds, where it helps grow more corn and so on and so on.

COMPANION PLANTING

When magma from volcanic eruptions in the deep ocean bubbles up through the surface water and cools to form a new island, the bare rock is initially devoid of life. Some of the first species to arrive are lichens, which are a symbiotic partnership between fungi and algae. The lichen's fungal body latches onto the barren rock, and the algae inside it photosynthesizes to generate food for them both from the sun's energy. As the lichens complete their life cycle and break down, their organic matter mixes with minerals in the rock to begin to form soil that can support the roots of plants, including mosses and grasses. Grass roots form thick mats that give structure to the soil, which allows it to support larger plants like bushes and trees. Some of these bushes and trees host beneficial bacteria in their roots that inject nitrogen into the soil to feed the grass. Over thousands of years, plants and animals cooperate to transform these islands from barren volcanic rock to lush forests, such as those found on the older Hawaiian and Galapagos Islands.

In the Pest Management chapter (page 35), we will discuss how competition, predation, and cooperation connect the plants, fungi, and critters in a garden's ecosystem. In this chapter, we're going to focus on our favorite of those three elements: cooperation. In some cases, our crops cooperate by actively helping one another—for example, providing a trellis in exchange for nutrients. In other cases, crops have such different needs that they grow right next to one another and share the soil in perfect harmony. We like to call these two types of garden companions "active companions" and "passive companions."

Active Companions

THREE SISTERS

The most well-known example of active companionship in the garden is the Three Sisters method. This Indigenous American style of growing corn, beans, and squash together has been used for thousands of years by different cultures

Three Sisters growing in harmony

across Mesoamerica, and for good reason. In this trio, the cornstalks provide tall structures for the beans to climb and access sunlight; the beans fertilize the soil when they break down at the end of the season by hosting nitrogen-fixing bacteria in their roots; and the wide, sprawling leaves of vining squash provide a natural mulch that retains moisture in the soil and suppresses weeds.

The key to growing a successful Three Sisters garden is to heed the instructions of its inventors. Many Indigenous cultures in North America didn't have a written language until the 21st century. Instead of writing their traditions, they told stories that contain important lessons, passing this information from one generation to the next. In the Haudenosaunee version of the Legend of the Three Sisters, three sisters live together in a field and care for one another deeply. The oldest sister, corn, stands tall and keeps watch over her other sisters. The middle sister, beans, darts back and forth through the arms of her older sister. The baby sister, squash, crawls low along the ground.

While this might just seem like a beautiful story of how these crops grow together, it contains important planting instructions for a Three Sisters garden. Corn grows the slowest of the three, so you need to plant it first for the stalks to grow large enough to support the beans—making it the oldest sister. When the corn is about a foot tall, you can seed your beans, and they will quickly begin to climb all over the cornstalks— classic middle child. Squash grows fastest of the three. If planted too soon, it would engulf and shade out the other two. After the corn has grown about 2 feet tall and the beans are just beginning to climb, plant your squash babies. If timed correctly, your Three Sisters patch will be one of the most hands-off and productive parts of your vegetable garden.

In 2022, we conducted a small experiment in two of our community garden plots. We grew Three Sisters plots side by side with conventional corn rows. At the end of the season, we harvested the plots and weighed the harvest. The Three Sisters plots and the conventional corn rows produced almost identical amounts of flour corn, but when we factored in the harvest of dry beans and winter squash, the Three Sisters plots produced significantly more food.

CARROTS AND RADISHES

A lesser-known example of active companionship is the partnership between radishes and carrots. Radishes germinate incredibly fast compared to slow-sprouting carrots, which can take weeks after planting to emerge. As every gardener knows, bare soil in your garden is an invitation for weeds. The carrot's slow germination leaves a lot of time for weeds to sprout, and before you know it, your carrot bed can become a tangled green mass of unwanted plants.

Growing fast-sprouting radishes between each row of carrots helps shade out weeds while the carrots take their time to sprout. By the time the carrots are rubbing elbows with the radishes, you harvest your radishes and the carrots fill in the empty space between the rows. This strategy not only suppresses weeds and helps the carrots, but it also provides a bonus harvest of radishes.

BRASSICAS AND OYSTER MUSHROOMS

Plants and fungi are old friends, and in many cases they literally cannot survive without one another. Healthy soil means plenty of fungi wrapping around the roots of our plants and providing them with water and nutrients in exchange for carbohydrates. Many of these helpful, soil-dwelling fungi don't produce edible mushrooms, but we can also use fungi above the soil to benefit our plants and grow edible mushrooms.

As we'll cover in more detail in the Oyster Mushrooms chapter (page 119), they can grow on pretty much any dead plant material. A few years ago, we were laying straw around our newly planted cabbage seedlings to suppress weeds and retain moisture, and it occurred to us that we were using that very same straw to grow oyster mushrooms in our basement. That spring, we decided to inoculate some of the straw with oyster mushrooms and then spread it around the base of the cabbage, kale, and collards. As the plants grew, their leaves provided shade to keep the oyster mushroom mycelium moist, and the mycelium broke down the straw to feed the cabbage, kale, and collards. The oysters eventually provided us with a small crop of delicious edible mushrooms in addition to beautiful, rich soil.

Passive Companions
TOMATOES AND BASIL

Passive companionship is often characterized by plants with such different growing habits and nutrient requirements that they don't even notice one another in the garden. Our favorite example is tomatoes and basil. The inspiration for this companionship started as a result of them being such a good pair on top of a pizza, but it blossomed into a real friendship in the garden. We often plant basil between rows of tomatoes, where it occupies the lower areas of the garden bed while the tomatoes are trellised

higher up. Other herbs, such as cilantro and parsley, also work well in tomato beds.

As we discuss in the Pest Management chapter (page 35), planting unrelated crops side by side can also help reduce pest pressure. The pungent aroma of basil can help mask the scent of tomatoes and even prevent pests from discovering your tomato crop!

PEPPERS AND ONIONS

Similar to tomatoes and basil, peppers and onions also make a famous pair in the kitchen and get along quite well in the garden. We line the lower, outer areas of our pepper beds with scallions and bulbing onions, while the peppers are trellised higher up.

Onions don't provide much for the peppers, and the peppers don't even notice the onions growing at their feet. Think of them like Craigslist roommates: They both benefit from splitting the rent, but they're not cooking dinner for each other.

This chapter covered tried-and-true companions, but don't be afraid to experiment with companion planting in your garden. Beans that like to climb cornstalks also do well with other tall plants, such as sunflowers and grain amaranth. Squash vines suppress weeds and retain moisture in other parts of the garden just like they do in the Three Sisters plots. Onions and herbs make nice, quiet roommates that can fit into most empty spaces among other veggies. We encourage you to try out different combinations! Imagine your garden beds as volcanic islands newly risen from the sea. Test which plants will cooperate to create a brand-new ecosystem.

COMPOSTING

Plants thrive in soil with added compost because the high levels of organic matter increase the retention of water and nutrients. Composting is also good for our planet because it helps reduce greenhouse gas emissions. When vegetable scraps, grass clippings, and even paper products go to landfills, they break down in an oxygen-free environment. When piled high and left to rot, the bacteria that break them down emit methane into the atmosphere, which is a powerful greenhouse gas. When these same materials break down in an oxygen-rich environment like a compost pile, the bacteria and fungi that break them down emit trace amounts of carbon dioxide, a far less powerful greenhouse gas than methane.

If your vegetable scraps and grass clippings go to landfills, they also carry valuable nutrients far from your garden, never to return again. Composting these materials keeps the nitrogen, phosphorus, potassium, and other nutrients cycling through your garden and contributes to a closed loop system. In addition to these nutrients, homemade compost also contains beneficial soil organisms and organic matter, and it helps amend heavy clay and sandy soils, bringing them into balance.

We use three types of composting to keep nutrients flowing through our gardens: cold composting, hot composting, and vermicomposting.

A cold compost heap

Turning compost

Cold Composting

Cold composting, sometimes called "no-rules composting," is the simplest method for home gardeners because you can add materials to the pile slowly over time. Choose a spot for the pile, and every time you add vegetable scraps, garden residue, or grass clippings, add a layer of dry leaves, straw, or other brown plant material as well. After several months or up to a year, the bottom of the pile will begin to look like usable compost. At that point, you can dig that out to use in your garden as needed, leaving the rest of the pile to continue breaking down.

Keep in mind that any fruit, vegetable, or unwanted weed seeds that enter your cold compost pile will remain viable when the compost is ready. The same is true of fungal plant diseases on spent garden plants. Be careful where you use this kind of finished compost to prevent spreading weed seeds and fungal plant disease in your garden beds.

Hot Composting

Hot composting is the most common method used by commercial growers and more advanced home gardeners because it produces usable compost in the shortest amount of time. Additionally, the heat generated during the process kills weed seeds and fungal plant diseases. In a hot compost system, you add all inputs into a pile at once rather than periodically over time. To start a hot compost pile, mix one-part dry, brown plant material, such as dead leaves, straw, or shredded paper, with one-part fresh, green plant material, such as grass clippings or vegetable scraps. Layer them in a pile with a base of at least 3 feet by 3 feet.

In this system, people sometimes refer to the brown material as "carbon" and the green material as "nitrogen." In reality, both elements are present in each of the materials, just in different amounts. Green leaves still have nitrogen in proteins and chlorophyll, while the brown leaves have leached most of that into the soil and primarily contain carbon. The pile of green and brown plant material creates the perfect environment for microorganisms that decompose plant material and form compost.

In this kind of compost pile, the life cycles of countless microorganisms generate heat, causing the piles to heat up to 160°F when the microbes are active. To keep track of the activity, you can simply stick your hand into the center of the pile at least once a week. If it feels hot, let it continue. When it starts to cool, turn the pile with a pitchfork or shovel to reintroduce oxygen and heat it back up. When watered and turned regularly, the turnaround time from plant material to usable compost with these piles can be as short as one month.

Vermicomposting

This third method doesn't offer the best option for large-scale composting, but when we were living in a small apartment with no yard, we composted all our kitchen scraps by feeding them to worms in a large plastic tub in our closet.

Vermicomposting most often uses red wigglers (*Eisenia fetida*), also called compost worms. They have a much more voracious appetite than the earthworms found in most North American gardens. You can order red wigglers online, and as long as you keep feeding them, you can grow your colony indefinitely. We have continued to upkeep our vermicompost bin in our basement for seven years. We have a small yard now, where we can compost our scraps outside, but in the winter, when our outdoor compost freezes solid, we switch to using our vermicompost bin.

To set up a vermicompost system, gather two lidded plastic containers of the same size. Drill or punch small holes in the side and bottom of one container to allow oxygen to flow and liquid to drain. The worms will live in this first container. Place it inside the second container, which will catch any liquid. Keep a lid on the bin because worms don't like sunlight. If the bin gets too moist and the worms start climbing up the sides, add a layer of dry material, such as shredded paper, straw, or leaves. You also can buy premade vermicompost bins online. If the worms are healthy and conditions in your bin are ade-

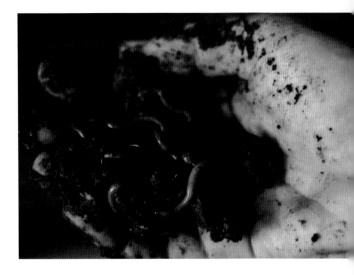

quate for them to survive, it should smell completely neutral.

With vermicomposting, the turnaround time from scraps to complete compost is relatively short. If you throw your scraps in an old blender before feeding them to your worms, it can be as short as a couple weeks.

Remember that each of these styles of composting is a colony of living organisms that requires oxygen and water to thrive. If you live in a particularly dry area, you will likely need to water your outdoor compost piles as often as you water your garden to keep them active. Once you get in the groove, composting your food scraps and garden waste will become second nature. Your garden and your planet will thank you!

PEST MANAGEMENT

If we ask you to close your eyes and picture an ecosystem, you'll probably visualize lions chasing wildebeests in the vast Kenyan savanna or colorful frogs snatching moths from the air in a Costa Rican rainforest, but less glamorous ecosystems exist everywhere that life exists. They include the spider that eats fruit flies in the corner of your kitchen ceiling and the insects that feed on pests in your garden. Predation, competition, and cooperation inextricably connect all organisms. This entire web of life—around us and inside us—makes up our ecosystem.

When Jordan finished his biology degree in 2013, he decided that, instead of getting a job at a laboratory or going to graduate school, he wanted to get a hands-on ecology education by completing an apprenticeship at a sustainable agriculture research farm in rural North Carolina. One July morning, he filled a backpack sprayer with pyrethrin, an organic pesticide, and walked into the misty fields to spray the Colorado potato beetles (*Leptinotarsa decemlineata*) that were decimating the potato crop. Colorado potato beetle larvae are plump red grubs that gnaw through potato foliage, leaving behind brown potato plant skeletons. In high enough numbers, they can kill entire fields of potatoes. That morning, the leaves Jordan expected to

find covered in feasting red grubs were instead dripping with red goo and buzzing with ravenous predatory wasps. He returned the backpack sprayer to the shed and turned to other chores because that morning the wasps had done the work for him.

The farm was using a method of pest control known as integrated pest management (IPM). Rather than the conventional method of attempting to kill *every living thing* in the fields with regular applications of broad-spectrum pesticides, IPM uses an ecosystem-focused approach to prevent crop damage. In a balanced ecosystem, predator numbers typically maintain healthy equilibrium at about 10 percent of the prey population. Imagine a potato patch with 500 potato beetles eating the leaves. A healthy version of this ecosystem would have 50 wasps preying on the beetles and keeping them in check. Imagine we spray that patch with conventional broad-spectrum pesticides. Those harsh chemicals might kill 99 out of every 100 insects in the patch, including the wasps. Statistically, the 1 percent of the insects that survived the pesticide application would leave five potato beetles and half a wasp. Half a wasp is a dead wasp, which means zero wasps. Those five surviving potato beetles would reproduce and quickly return to their original population of 500. But with no wasps around to keep the beetle population in check, those 500 beetles could quickly turn to 5,000, and the only option would be to spray the plants again and again to control them.

IPM, the pest management method we prefer, considers environmental conditions, such as beneficial insect habitat and garden cleanliness, to manage pests. IPM systems don't put pesticides off-limits but typically use them as a last resort to target specific pest species rather than *all* insects. Over our decade-plus of growing food together, we've seen firsthand evidence that this minimalist approach offers the most effective method of controlling pests and supporting the general health of our ecosystems—especially for small-scale growing operations, such as home gardens and small farms.

Managing pests naturally requires you to think more like an ecologist than a factory manager. Factories want everything precise and sterile so anyone can replicate the processes exactly the same way each time. But ecosystems almost never work this way. IPM creates a balanced ecosystem in which predators and plant diversity reduce pest damage to tolerable levels rather than eradicating pests entirely. The five primary tools we use to keep pest levels tolerable in our gardens are: polyculture planting, beneficial insect habitat, physical barriers, garden cleanliness, and, when needed, organic pesticides.

Polyculture Planting

In this method of food production, a diverse array of crops grow side by side rather than in giant blocks where every plant in the field is the same. Most home gardens are by their very nature a polyculture. For a good example of the alternative, a monoculture, think about the vast fields of corn or soybeans that blanket the North American countryside.

When a pest or disease comes upon a monoculture, it can run rampant and rapidly expand its population. Every plant in the field can serve as a suitable host, so it takes almost no time for those pests or diseases to spread from plant to plant, causing massive crop damage. In polycultures, the mix of different crops and varieties of those crops, some resistant to specific pests and diseases, disrupts that rapid expansion. In some cases, this prevents them from finding their target crop entirely.

The Colorado potato beetles we discussed earlier are specialist herbivores that only eat the leaves of nightshade plants, primarily potatoes. If we interplant our potato rows with beets, cabbage, and carrots, the potato beetles will have a much harder time finding their host plants as they traverse the garden. If they land on a carrot top, then a cabbage leaf, they might even decide that your garden has no suitable plants for their larvae there and fly off elsewhere.

Beneficial Insect Habitat

Beneficial insects are another very important element of managing pests in the garden. Often when gardeners think of beneficial insects, they picture bees and other pollinators. While pollinators are incredibly important for aiding in fruit production, when it comes to pest management, predatory insects are the real stars.

Ladybugs, parasitoid wasps, lacewings, and other predatory insects function as the gray wolves or lions of the insect world, maintaining balanced ecosystems in gardens by preying on herbivorous insects. (Quick vocab lesson: "parasitoid" means the predator kills the host; "parasitic" means it doesn't.) Each ladybug or lacewing can eat up to 75 aphids per day. A handful of ladybugs might not eradicate the aphids from your garden, but the little red beauties will keep pest populations lower, which will help avoid more significant damage to the plants.

Voracious tomato hornworms can defoliate an entire tomato plant in a matter of days. Luckily, parasitoid wasps can keep them in check. If you find hornworms with rows of white cocoons on their backs, wasps have more or less zombified them, and their bodies are serving as nurseries for wasp larvae. That may sound kind of horrifying, but the wasps' work keeping tomato hornworms and other pest caterpillars in check is crucial for organic tomato production.

Some companies propagate and sell beneficial insects for gardeners, but many of the insects they sell are native to North America and likely

A pollinator garden

already exist in your area. The best way to attract these beneficial insects is by maintaining their preferred habitat nearby. We do this with a pollinator garden that includes fennel, cilantro, dill, and native wildflowers, such as goldenrod, yarrow, and milkweed. As adults, parasitoid wasps feed on the nectar and pollen of these plants, so having them in or near your garden means harnessing the zombifying power of the wasps. Ladybugs, lacewings, praying mantises, and other predatory insects will also use the habitat provided by these wildflowers to rear their young and keep their populations healthy around your garden.

Physical Barriers

There's probably no more surefire way to prevent pest damage in your vegetable garden than using physical barriers to keep pests from accessing your crops in the first place and turning them into an outdoor salad bar. White-tailed deer love the environments that humans create, especially suburbs and farmland. The parts of Pittsburgh where we grow our food sometimes feel like they have as many deer as people. If not for the 6-foot fence surrounding our community garden, they would happily chew everything to the ground. In other regions, rabbits pose more of a problem. For them, lower, half-buried chicken-wire fences offer the best protection.

Physical barriers can also help prevent damage from insects. The cabbage white butterfly (*Pieris rapae*) loves to prey on brassicas, including cabbage, kale, collards, and broccoli. These small butterflies flutter around, searching for suitable plants on which to lay their eggs. Butterflies have taste buds on their feet called "contact chemoreceptors," which allow them to identify host plants by landing on them. We use floating row covers suspended over our brassica beds by wire hoops to prevent the butterflies from discovering them, which allows us to grow lush, hole-free greens without pesticides.

Physical barriers like floating row covers can prevent beneficial insects, including pollinators, from accessing your garden, too, so this tech-

Row covers

nique works great for greens and root vegetables, which don't need pollinating insects to produce a crop. If we covered our squash plants for the entire season, we'd have a pristine, bug-free patch of unpollinated, fruitless squash vines!

Garden Cleanliness

The phrase *garden cleanliness* is a bit of a misnomer because your garden shouldn't be "clean." Healthy gardens are teeming with all types of life: plants, insects, fungi, and bacteria. In this sense, the concept of cleanliness means disrupting the life cycle of insect pests by removing dead plant material from the garden, then composting it in a hot compost pile or burning it.

When insect pests suddenly appear in your garden, it seems as though they all must have flown in overnight. But many of them were lying in wait in your garden debris all winter long. Many insect pests survive the winter by burrowing into garden waste like dead cornstalks, old squash vines, and piles of dead bean plants. To disrupt their life cycle, remove this debris from your garden at the end of the season and apply heat to it through a hot compost pile, which will kill the overwintering pests. Composting this garden waste won't eradicate all the pests from your garden, but it will set them back come springtime and give your crops a significant head start.

Organic Pesticides

Even in a well-balanced garden with a healthy ecosystem, you will still have occasional outbreaks of certain insect pests. When this happens, you have two choices: lose the crop or spray pesticides. Because we rely on our gardens for a significant amount of the food we eat, we can't risk losing our main crops to insect pests. In 2023, we had a large outbreak of Mexican bean beetles (*Epilachna varivestis*) in our Cherokee black beans. These beans are one of our main staple crops through the winter, so we chose to spray the bean beetles with the organic pesticide pyrethrin.

Although pyrethrin is an organic pesticide

made from chrysanthemum flowers and it deteriorates in a matter of days after applying it, it is still a broad-spectrum insecticide that will kill almost any insect it touches. In the rare cases that we use it, we spray pyrethrin in a very targeted fashion and avoid spraying when pollinators and predatory insects are most active. Bees and wasps do most of their work in the afternoon, and butterflies and dragonflies around midday, so we sprayed the pest beetles early in the morning.

Other organic pesticides, such as *Bacillus thuringiensis*, commonly called "Bt," target only certain types of insects. Bt is a bacteria-based pesticide that specifically affects caterpillars, which makes it safe to spray around most beneficial insects because the bacteria doesn't affect them.

We also occasionally use insecticidal soap, which is highly effective at reducing aphid populations when the ladybugs and lacewings can't keep up. Like Bt, insecticidal soap is a targeted pesticide that will only kill soft-bodied insects like aphids and whiteflies, so it's generally safe to use around beneficial insects.

Particular pests affect specific crops, so we'll come back to these principles in each crop chapter. In the meantime, we want you to understand that your garden is an ecosystem, not a factory. It's not your job to sterilize and control every aspect of it but, rather, to set it up for success and allow it to thrive naturally. When you manage your garden like an ecosystem and accept the help of all your garden allies, problems often take care of themselves or don't arise at all.

WEED MANAGEMENT

Ah weeds, the bane of every gardener's existence. So many aspiring gardeners eagerly start their first garden only to give up in despair in the middle of the season as unwanted plants pop up and choke out their crops as soon as they turn their backs. But it doesn't have to be that way. Over the years of farming and gardening, we've collected a toolbox of techniques for making weeds a nonissue in our garden. That way, we can get back to the fun part: watching plants grow and reaping the harvest.

First, let's define a weed. Many plants classified as "weeds" in American gardens are wild, edible, nutritious, delicious plants. Take amaranth, also known as pigweed. In fields across the country, commercial corn and soybean growers probably spray millions of gallons of herbicide on this "noxious weed" each year. But amaranth, a wild cousin of spinach, has the same impressive nutritional profile and flavor. In our gardens, although we don't plant it intentionally, "pigweed" is not a weed. We let it grow undis-

turbed as long as it doesn't get in the way of our primary crops, then pick it when it's nice and bushy for a bonus harvest. Simply put, which plants are "weeds" and which plants are "bonus harvests" is completely up to you. If a plant starts growing in your garden and you don't want it there, for whatever reason, it's a weed. If you're OK with it, it's not a weed.

Most plants considered weeds reproduce quickly in huge numbers. From just one plant, pigweed disperses thousands of seeds that

quickly germinate to take over bare soil. That property makes it excellent for erosion control, holding valuable topsoil in place and keeping soil biology strong through photosynthesis and long taproots. In a scenario where a piece of land has been torn to shreds by a tiller or flattened by earth movers for a new development, many of the plants we consider weeds are the first ones on the scene. They operate like first responders to limit the ecological damage and hold the soil in place so it doesn't blow away in the wind or wash away in the rain. Because our vegetable gardens also contain a lot of disturbed soil, the qualities that make weedy plants so helpful in ecosystem recovery can make them a major nuisance in our garden beds. For keeping annual weeds at bay, one of the best things you can do is minimize soil disturbance by using low-till or no-till gardening practices.

Low-Till and No-Till Growing

Tilling soil destroys the roots of most plants, making it a common way to eradicate weeds. You may need to do so when opening a new garden space, and some gardeners till every spring in preparation for planting. But the downside to this method is that tilling churns up weed seeds previously buried too deep to sprout. Certain weeds, such as bindweed and thistles, also spread through root fragments, so by tilling you may be inadvertently spreading them throughout the garden, making the problem worse than before.

We prefer to eradicate weeds by restricting their sunlight, smothering them with cardboard or a silage tarp before planting our main crop. We use manufactured silage tarps because they don't degrade with UV exposure, unlike typical tarps from a hardware store. All garden weeds require photosynthesis, so this method kills everything that has sprouted in the garden. In the cool temperatures of early spring, the smothering takes three to four weeks. Warm weather accelerates the process, though, so it takes only two weeks in the heat of summer. Check the progress every week or so, and when the weeds have turned fully brown and are starting to decay, remove the tarp or cardboard and plant your main crop. This method leaves buried weed seeds too deep in the soil to sprout and significantly reduces the number of weeds that will pop up during the growing season.

Weeding during the Season

No matter how well you eradicate weeds before planting, a few will pop up here and there while your crops are growing. Keep them in check by hoeing them lightly when they first emerge. A few weeks after planting our crops, we keep an eye out, and as soon as we see a few weed sprouts emerging, we scrape them down with a flat hoe. This strategy kills the weeds that were close enough to the surface to sprout without turning up new seeds from deep in the soil. After that initial weeding, the main crops often grow fast enough to shade out the next round of weeds.

You can also pile on mulch to smother weeds as the growing season progresses. We do this in our dedicated bean rows, where we have to deal with some aggressive grass weeds. Each spring, we pile about 4 inches of woodchip mulch— left by arborists at our community garden—in the rows between our bean vines. The mulch keeps the grass under control long enough for the beans to shade the weeds out and produce a healthy crop by the time the grass breaks through the mulch. As the mulch breaks down, it also produces a beautiful, dark compost that keeps the soil healthy and replenished.

Managing Weeds Offseason

At the end of the season, when you're done harvesting your crops, you might feel tempted to compost all the leftover plant matter and call it a day, but that would be a mistake. Remember, bare soil is an open invitation to weeds, and many of them can survive just fine in the offseason, whether that be winter or dry weather. They may grow slowly at first, but after conditions improve, they will have established themselves, ready to take over right when you're about to sow your spring seeds. The best way to prevent spring weed headaches is with cover crops.

In the Bed Prep chapter (page 16), we discussed the many benefits to using cover crops, including their ability to outcompete weeds. When a thick bed of rye, oats, and clover covers your garden soil, weed seeds no longer have bare soil to take advantage of. Some cover crops, such as rye, even excrete compounds from their roots that discourage the germination of weed seeds. In the fall, we like to plant a cover crop of clover and winter rye that establishes itself over the winter and prevents weeds from taking over. Then, in the spring, we can easily smother the cover crop with a silage tarp and use it as a green mulch for our main crops.

Employing these good weed-management strategies will help ensure your garden is as hands-off and productive as possible. Taking the initiative and putting a weed-management strategy in place from the start can mean the difference between battling a weed-filled nightmare and enjoying thriving beds of healthy crops.

PROCESSING AND STORING YOUR HARVEST

On a late summer evening, the sun seems to take hours to make up its mind and set. A symphony of crickets and katydids scores the slow, almost imperceptible lengthening of shadows. We're strolling around the garden, deciding what to make for dinner based on what catches our eyes. A bright red tomato is at the perfect stage—bulbous and soft—and we snip it into the harvest basket along with a large bunch of parsley and a handful of sweet peppers and green beans. Our meal-planning wheels are spinning now, and we can see flatbreads piled with grilled veggies drizzled in tahini.

For us, that's the meal-prep ideal: having a bounty at our disposal and letting inspiration strike. But for love and family, we've made our home in Pittsburgh, where scenes like the one above are only possible for about half the year. Luckily, we've discovered the next best thing to a garden brimming with possibility, and that's a pantry brimming with preserves.

During much of human history, eating fresh vegetables year-round was impossible. Much of the world's population lives in temperate climates that have dormant seasons when plants grow slowly or not at all. Nomadic hunter-gatherers could travel from place to place, following the water, plants, and animals that sustained them. After the invention of agriculture, people developed ways to preserve their harvest bounty and nourish themselves through the winter while staying put. Go to any grocery store and you can still see these same preservation techniques being used today in the form of fermented foods, fruit leather, pickles, and more. In our household, we preserve our garden harvest with

those techniques, allowing us to keep home-grown meals on our plates year-round.

Canning

Best for: tomatoes, sweet peppers, acidic fruits

When you imagine preserving a garden harvest, canning probably comes to mind first. It's funny that in this day and age canning is largely viewed as the purview of grandmothers of yesteryear in frilly aprons, when it's actually one of the most cutting-edge, scientific preservation methods available. It's also the newest of the techniques in this chapter, invented only in the early 1800s. The French government offered a cash prize for anyone able to come up with a good way to preserve fruits and vegetables long-term for use in soldiers' rations. French confectioner Nicolas Appert discovered that, by sealing produce in jars so oxygen couldn't reach it and boiling the contents, the food resisted spoilage.

Since then, the techniques and equipment used in canning have gone through several evolutions, but the general process has remained the same. Appert didn't know the hard science about microbes causing spoilage, but we now understand what makes canning such an effective method. Boiling the food destroys the mold, yeast, and bacteria responsible for spoiling the food. Keeping it sealed without access to air prevents new spoilers from getting in and taking hold. It's pretty innovative!

However, boiling temperatures alone don't destroy one common bacteria that thrives in an oxygen-free environment like a sealed jar and can produce a dangerous toxin. *Clostridium botulinum*, the boogeyman bacterium of all aspiring home canners, causes botulism. When we started canning, we rightfully feared botulism because it's undetectable by taste and can lead to serious illness or even death. Learning how canning works and following the guidelines recommended by the USDA and the National Center for Home Food Preservation (www.nchfp.uga .edu) have made us confident in preserving our food without fear of botulism. As long as you follow their recommended safety procedures correctly, you should feel confident, too.

Water-bath canning heats jars to boiling for long enough that the entire contents of the jars reach 212°F, which destroys microbes that could spoil it. Botulism spores can survive boiling temperatures, so the only way to water-bath can safely is by choosing foods acidic enough that botulinum bacteria can't grow in or on them. Many fruits naturally fall below that threshold: 4.6 on the pH scale, which measures acidity and alkalinity. (You can look up which fruits fall below this threshold on the website of the National Center for Home Food Preservation.) For foods that are not acidic enough, which includes most garden vegetables, such as green beans, peppers, and potatoes, you can acidify them with vinegar, lemon juice, or ascorbic acid.

You can also preserve low-acidity foods through pressure canning, which heats the contents of the jars above the boiling point of water, thereby destroying all botulinum bacteria. The National Center for Home Food Preservation's website offers safe, tested recipes for both these methods of canning, as do specific cookbooks, such as the *Ball Blue Book Guide to Preserving* or *Putting Food By*.

You don't need much specialized equipment to begin water-bath canning, but some necessary supplies and tools will make your life easier. To water-bath can safely, you need canning jars—the classic, three-piece Mason-style jars are our go-to—and a large pot with a lid. The pot should be deep enough that you can fill it with enough water to cover the tops of your jars by 2 inches. Rather than placing the jars directly on the bottom of the pot, where they will clank around and possibly break, set them on a short wire rack or a dish towel placed in the pot. A ladle and metal funnel will help get your produce into the jars without making a big mess, and a jar lifter, a pair of tongs designed to pick up canning jars, is very useful for getting your jars into and out of the hot water.

At room temperature, properly canned veggies and fruits will remain shelf-stable for years.

Dehydrating

Best for: mushrooms, tomatoes, hot peppers, herbs, fruit, dry beans, grain corn

Like all living things, the bacteria and fungi responsible for causing vegetables to rot need water to survive. Dehydrating vegetables saves space in your freezer and refrigerator, and it makes your produce small and lightweight, perfect for taking on hiking or camping trips or bringing to work as a snack. The method does have some drawbacks, however. The fruit or vegetable loses some nutritional value, and the process can change the ingredient's texture dramatically—sometimes a plus for fruit! A chewy bite into concentrated sugars makes a great snack.

If you live in a very arid climate, simply use the air and sun to dry your harvests. Slice veggies into thin strips and hang them on wires or lay them on well-ventilated shelves, making sure to protect them from any critters looking for an easy meal. On the rare occasions it's dry enough to do this where we live, we put mesh screens over our produce to keep birds and bugs away. In humid environments, fruits or vegetables with a high moisture content will likely rot before they can dry thoroughly. We use a dehydrator, which allows us to control the temperature. It has several racks and a built-in fan that constantly circulates hot air over the produce, reducing drying time considerably. If you don't want to invest in a dehydrator, putting your oven on its lowest setting and leaving the door slightly cracked is a decent alternative, though not as efficient.

To make dehydrated fruits and vegetables shelf-stable, they need to be "cracker dry," meaning dry enough that, when you bend them, they snap like a cracker. When you press into the surface with a fingernail, you should see no moisture on the outside. After they've reached the target state, seal them in airtight containers so they don't reabsorb moisture from the air. We store our dehydrated vegetables in glass canning jars with airtight lids, a perfect way to reuse old canning lids because you shouldn't can with lids more than once.

In addition to the foods listed at the beginning of this section, we occasionally chop and dry other vegetables, including potatoes and onions, for backpacking trips since the process makes them so light. After you've put your dried food into containers, check them in a day or two for condensation forming on the jar. If any forms, your food didn't dry enough to store properly. You need to dehydrate it further and try again. It's much better to catch condensation early than to grab a jar from the pantry only to discover that fuzzy mold has covered its contents—trust us!

At room temperature, properly dehydrated vegetables will remain shelf-stable indefinitely, though they'll lose some flavor over time.

Pickling

Best for: cucumbers, squash, peppers, beets, radishes, turnips

Lowering the pH of your vegetables can make the environment so inhospitable to bacteria and fungi that they simply can't survive. Pickling takes this method to the extreme. Pickled vegetables use a vinegar brine to significantly lower the pH, usually to between 3 and 4 on the pH scale. Pickling can serve as a precursor to canning in that vegetables you normally wouldn't water-bath can, such as green beans or carrots, are acidified in a brine to the point where they can be safely canned. You can also use pickling to extend the shelf life of veggies in the fridge. With all that time in boiling water, canning pickled vegetables often results in softer textures, so we reserve it for marinated peppers and other foods where softness is a virtue. We keep the pickled vegetables that we want to stay crisp, like cucumbers, turnips, and radishes, in the fridge. A good, basic brine for refrigerator pickles consists of equal parts vinegar and water, with 1 tablespoon of salt per cup of liquid and a little bit of sugar to taste. Customize your brine with whatever herbs and spices sound good with the vegetable you're pickling. Dill and garlic make an obvious choice for pickled cucumbers, but there's a whole world of flavors to explore.

COLD BRINING

This is the simplest form of pickling, where you simply add your fruits or vegetables to a solution of vinegar, water, and spices and keep the mixture in the fridge. You can even make a big batch of pickling brine to keep in the fridge so you always have some on hand for unexpected gluts of garden produce. Cold brine takes a little longer to penetrate the food, so you'll want to wait a day or two before eating your pickles. The veggies stay raw, so this method keeps them crisper.

HOT BRINING

In this method, you slice your vegetables and pack them into clean jars. Then boil your brine ingredients, pour the hot liquid into the jars, seal them, and let them cool to room temperature before refrigerating them. You can store hot-brined veggies in the fridge for several months. We've had jars of pickles around for much longer, and they've lasted perfectly fine. Over time, however, they'll soften and their flavor will diminish. Hot-brine pickling works especially well for harder vegetables, such as carrots and radishes, because the heat slightly cooks the vegetables, making them more tender.

Fermenting

Best for: cabbage, hot peppers

Most preservation methods seek to fight bacterial growth, but with fermentation we use beneficial bacteria to our advantage. Fermentation is sometimes referred to as "controlled rot" because this process allows safe bacteria, such as *Lactobacillus*, to break down our fruits and vegetables in such a way that it creates an acidic environment that other bacteria and fungi find inhospitable. Our favorite method for preserving vegetables is lactic acid fermentation. *Lactobacillus* are naturally present on untreated fresh produce, so to ferment homegrown foods, you essentially just need to create an environment the bacteria can thrive in. Luckily for us, *Lactobacillus* tolerate salt while harmful bacteria generally don't. One easy way to encourage the good growth and stifle the bad is by putting produce into a brine that is 2 percent to 5 percent salt by weight. The salt will pull the liquid out of the vegetables.

Fermentation is an ancient form of preservation used all over the world, so there is an incredible array of traditions and flavors to choose from when deciding how to best preserve your vegetables. For example, if you are growing cabbage, you could preserve it using a traditional German method and make sauerkraut (which translates to "sour cabbage"), or you could follow the Korean example and turn it into spicy, funky kimchi. All you need to get started fermenting is some produce, salt, and a nonreactive container, like a ceramic crock or jar, to put it in. We use Mason jars for smaller batches and a 1-gallon ceramic crock for bigger projects.

Freezing

Best for: leafy greens, fruit, peppers

We're very grateful for the ability to freeze our food. We have both a stand-up freezer and a chest freezer in our basement, and by the time winter rolls around, both are completely full of garden produce and foraged food. At harvest, it's very convenient to throw produce in the freezer without having to dehydrate or can it first, and the flavor and nutrients stay close to harvest levels. Despite its simplicity, there are some distinctions and guidelines to keep in mind when freezing your garden bounty.

Bags of frozen peppers

First, keeping produce in your freezer doesn't kill fungi or bacteria, but it does prevent them from spreading throughout your food over time as they would in warmer temperatures. So you should freeze fruits and vegetables in prime condition, with no signs of mold or rot. If a food item is starting to turn, freezing it won't fix the situation.

Freezing also doesn't destroy or stop the natural enzymes in vegetables that initiate decomposition. The cold will slow them, yes, but it won't stop them completely. If left long enough, those enzymes will degrade the texture, color, and flavor of a lot of produce, even if it was perfectly fresh when frozen. If you've ever frozen fresh green beans and later defrosted them to find a slimy brown pile of mush, you can blame those enzymes. Blanching your vegetables before freezing—by briefly submerging them in boiling water, then quickly cooling them—will destroy those enzymes and give them a better taste and texture down the line. We blanch and freeze big piles of collards, spinach, kale, peas, green beans, and sweet corn every year.

As a general rule, produce with a high water content doesn't freeze well. At the very least, its texture will change dramatically. But don't let that stop you from getting creative if you have a bumper crop of something that traditionally "doesn't freeze." Silvan's mom has been making and freezing lettuce and potato soup for years now, and though we were initially reluctant to try it, it's really good!

To preserve herbs that lose their flavor when dried, such as basil and cilantro, we finely chop or blend them with olive oil and freeze the mixture in small chunks. Ice cube trays work great for this. Fruit generally freezes well without blanching first, but we like to spread it on a baking sheet and let it freeze solid before transferring it into plastic freezer bags. This method keeps the fruit from freezing into a giant, solid block that requires an ice pick to break apart.

Curing

Best for: winter squash, potatoes, sweet potatoes, carrots, beets, cabbages, garlic, onions

The most basic form of preserving vegetables is curing. The crops that work well with this method are ones specifically bred to store—think winter squash, potatoes, sweet potatoes, garlic, onions, etc. These crops are full of water and, though fully alive, go more or less dormant over the winter. They store by their very nature. The key to curing storage vegetables properly is to allow them to reach full maturity on the plant, then store them in their ideal conditions. Some storage crops, like carrots, beets, and cabbages, do best in a cold, humid environment. We don't have nearly enough room in our refrigerator to hold the root crops we save for winter, so we put them in perforated plastic bags inside waxed cardboard boxes in the garage. Traditional root-cellar guides often suggest packing root vegetables in layers of moist sand, soil, or leaves in buckets, which is another excellent option. Luckily, our garage tends to stay humid and just above freezing in winter.

Other storage crops need warmer, somewhat drier conditions. Our storage pumpkins and winter squash hang out happily on our mantel and windowsills all year, as long as we picked them after they had developed a thick skin and hard stem. Potatoes also need warmer temperatures than root crops. Their ideal conditions are ventilated but dark: a wire shelf or basket in a cabinet or a basement without windows. Any light will induce the potatoes to sprout. The same rule holds true for garlic and onions, which we store in hanging mesh baskets in our basement.

Perusing the jars in our pantry and digging through our freezers full of fruits and veggies comes a close second to wandering through the garden itself, looking for dinner inspiration. We still rejoice when spring returns and we can eat straight from the garden again, but with the variety of preservation techniques available, we love eating homegrown food year-round!

SEED SAVING

Years ago, a farmer friend of Silvan's mom, Sarah, gifted her a pumpkin with deep ridges, the seeds of which she used to start her own pumpkin patch. A few years later, Sarah gave us a beautiful tan pumpkin she had grown in her North Carolina garden. From that gift, we set aside a few seeds and roasted the rich, orange flesh. The next spring, we planted some of the seeds in our community garden in Pittsburgh, where they produced massive vines that sprawled in all directions. By late fall, very few of the pumpkins were maturing, though, likely because they were expecting the long North Carolina growing season. We harvested only a couple of ripe pumpkins; the rest succumbed to the Pennsylvania frost. We saved seeds from the pumpkin vines that matured early and grew them in that same community garden plot the next year. The next time, a few more of them ripened before the frost came. Over the years, we've repeated that pattern, and now almost all the pumpkins ripen before the frost ends our growing season.

The pumpkins have adapted to our shorter growing season because the vines that produced pumpkins that matured early passed on their genes in mature seeds. Those that grew too slowly didn't. That story probably feels a little like high school biology class because the process we're describing is Natural Selection. Long before Charles Darwin visited the Galapagos Islands or Gregor Mendel crossbred his pea plants, humans were naturally selecting and eating plants with desirable traits, such as big fruits and tasty leaves. Our gardening ancestors planted the seeds from the tastiest plants to grow the next year. Over thousands of years, this process transformed plants like corn from a spindly wild grass called teosinte into thick, 12-foot-tall stalks with ears that can weigh a pound each. Drastic changes like that happen over thousands of years at the hands of many generations of farmers and gardeners, but within our own gardens we can use seed saving to nudge our crops in the right direction.

Saving seeds also preserves the genetic variation of heirloom varieties of vegetables and fruits. While large commercial tomato farms are growing the latest hybrid tomato varieties—bred for bright red skin and pale, sour flesh that can withstand being jostled around in a tractor trailer—small farmers and home gardeners maintain flavorful heirloom varieties like Cherokee Purple, Amish Paste, and Brandywine. We take part in a seed swap every March at our local library, where people from around Pittsburgh donate bags of seeds they've saved from their gardens and leftover seeds from heirloom seed companies. The bags of seeds are labelled, organized and laid out on long tables from which hundreds of people from around town take as many as they like to grow in their own vegetable gardens.

Seed swaps have an immense impact on preserving heirloom varieties. If we donate a bag of 100 black bean seeds from some plants that did well in our garden and 10 people take home 10 seeds each, they can easily produce 100 new

Saving Carolina Princess Pumpkin seeds

bean seeds per plant over the next growing season. That means the 100 black beans we shared could become 10,000 bean seeds to share with other growers or use for food in just one season. If our community repeated this process for four growing seasons, it would result in 100 billion bean seeds! We enjoy sharing gardening knowledge on social media, but that's the type of "going viral" we find most exciting.

When teaching new gardeners how to save seeds, we like to break the process into three categories of difficulty. Level one seeds come from crops in which the part of the plant harvested as food contains the mature seed. Level two seeds come from crops typically harvested underripe; they need to overgrow to yield mature seeds. Level three seeds come from biennial crops, which take two growing seasons to produce mature seeds. Let's take a closer look at each of the levels.

Level One Seed Saving

Examples: flour corn, popcorn, dry beans, dry peas, winter squash, tomatoes, peppers

As you might imagine, it's easiest to save seeds from the part of the plant that we're already harvesting for food anyway. It's simple to save seeds from dry beans, dry peas, flour corn, and popcorn because you just avoid eating a handful of them and plant them the next year. You can just grab a scoop of random seeds to save, but if you want to improve the variety year over year, you should try to observe the plants while they grow and mark a few of the healthiest plants to save seeds from.

Mature fruits like winter squash, tomatoes, and peppers also contain ripe seeds. With these plants, you usually need to remove some of the fruit flesh from the seeds before drying them to store for next season. It's important to ensure that these fruits are fully ripe before you try to save seeds from them. A green tomato or green pepper likely won't have fully mature seeds, so let them ripen fully before harvesting them and saving seeds. The best method for cleaning the seeds off is to place them on a screen or in a mesh colander, run clean water over them, then lay them on a paper towel or plate, moving them around once a day until they dry completely.

Level Two Seed Saving

Examples: sweet corn, green beans, summer squash, snap peas, spinach

Growers pick crops such as sweet corn, green beans, and summer squash young, with underdeveloped and tender seeds. This property makes them pleasant to eat fresh, but leaves you with no viable seeds to produce new plants the next year. Other crops, including spinach and arugula, haven't flowered yet when we harvest them. In other words, you can't have your spinach seeds and eat it, too. To collect seeds from these plants, simply leave them in the garden beds long past when you would normally harvest them to allow them to produce mature seeds.

With some fruits left on each plant, sweet corn, green beans, and summer squash will mature, similar to their level one counterparts. Then you can collect the mature seeds and treat them just like level one seeds. As the weather warms, spinach, arugula, and other leafy greens will "bolt," meaning they transition from leafy growth to producing flowers, then tender, green seed pods. After the seed pods become brown and dry, you can collect them in a bag and store them, as they are, to replant next season.

Level Three Seed Saving

Examples: carrots, beets, cabbage, kale, collards, onions

The process of saving seeds from these plants isn't complicated, but it is inconvenient. They're biennials, meaning they take two growing seasons to produce seeds. To save seeds from level three plants, you'll need to occupy valuable growing space for two seasons to grow a plant you can't eat. For people with limited space, it probably isn't worth it to save seeds from level three plants. If you do have some extra space, though, these plants behave similarly to the spinach and arugula mentioned in the previous section—except you need to winterize them with row covers or heavy mulch to make sure you don't lose them to the frost. If they survive the winter, let them flower and produce seeds, then collect the seeds when the pods turn brown and dry.

Cross-Pollination

On the surface, it's pretty straightforward to save seeds from plants like corn and squash. The difficulty lies in preventing cross-pollination between varieties. Corn is wind-pollinated, which means that, if you're gardening in an area with a lot of corn production or you're growing multiple varieties in close proximity, the different varieties will likely cross-pollinate, which is essentially rolling the dice on the genetic lottery. Plants grown from seeds saved from cross-pollinated plants might not resemble the parent plant you wanted to propagate. Squash and pumpkins are a little less prone to cross-pollinating, but because insects pollinate them, they can cross-pollinate with other squash varieties nearby. One year, we accidentally crossed our winter squash with a summer squash, and the next year half our winter squash tasted watery and flavorless. We tossed those seeds and replanted some of the original winter squash seeds the next year, keeping them far away from the summer squash.

If you're growing multiple varieties of corn or squash near one another, avoid cross-pollination by hand-pollinating your plants then marking the not-crossed fruit from which to save seeds. The simplest way to save seeds from crops prone to cross-pollination is to physically isolate the different varieties. We have a small garden space at our house, and we also rent large community garden plots. We grow our Hopi Blue flour corn at the house and our Wapsie Valley dent corn at the community gardens to keep them from cross-pollinating. You can approximate the same method with windbreaks, such as a hedgerow, tall wooden fence, or house separating the varieties.

Beans, peas, tomatoes, and peppers are primarily self-pollinated, so they're much less likely to cross-pollinate with other varieties. Insects sometimes spread pollen from one plant to another, though, so separating varieties by at least 10 feet will significantly decrease the likelihood of cross-pollination, though you still may get a few surprises from time to time.

Storing Seeds

At room temperature, all seeds remain viable for at least one or two years, but you can extend their life by storing them in airtight containers in your refrigerator. We use small glass jelly jars or plastic pill organizers to store our seeds, and we've dedicated one of the crisper drawers in our refrigerator as our personal "seed vault." In those conditions, most of the seeds could probably stay viable for five to six years, though the germination rate—the percentage that sprouted—would decrease every year after that. To keep germination rates high, we replenish the seed vault every year or two with fresh seeds from the garden. That way we don't have to save seeds from every crop every year to keep our seed stock full.

At this point, you might be thinking, *Saving seeds seems like* a lot *of extra work when I can easily order heirloom seeds from the companies mentioned in the Seed Sourcing chapter*, and you know what . . . you're right! Seed saving definitely isn't a beginner gardener activity. If you're feeling overwhelmed by it this year, skip this process entirely. In a couple years, when this book is dirty and full of marked pages, come back to this chapter and give it a try. Alternatively, if you're feeling inspired to save your own seeds this year, remember that you're taking part in a human tradition that goes back more than 10,000 years, and the 100 seeds you save from your garden this year could become 100 billion seeds around your community a few years from now.

PART TWO

CROPS

BEANS

Per Pound Dry
CALORIES: 1,500   **CARBS:** 164 g   **PROTEIN:** 110 g   **FAT:** 6.5 g
IMPORTANT MICRONUTRIENTS: potassium, iron, calcium

If you're flipping through this book, searching for a crop that is nutritionally dense, easy to preserve, and easy to grow, flip no further. Mature dry beans are packed with protein, carbohydrates, and dietary fiber, making them a critical part of our staple crop repertoire. They can be stored indefinitely at room temperature, so they don't require valuable freezer space. Additionally, beans host beneficial bacteria in their roots that pull nitrogen from the air and convert it into a form that can be used to fuel plant growth, so just growing beans in your garden improves the soil!

Beans are thought to have been first cultivated alongside their traditional sister crops, corn and squash, about 7,000 years ago in what is now southern Mexico. Over thousands of years, they were brought north along trade routes, with unique varieties being developed along the way. From their initial cultivation, beans have served as a vital staple crop for people in the Americas and, more recently, around the world. Chickpeas were first cultivated about 12,000 years ago in what is now western Jordan and southern Syria. Although they are a different species from American dry beans, we included them in this chapter because their growing conditions and use as food are so similar to their American cousins.

We grow gallons and gallons of dry beans every year to eat throughout the winter. In the depths of our frigid Pennsylvania winters, one of our favorite meals to eat is a big pot of slow-cooked black beans and hominy. We usually add venison to the pot, but if you eat a plant-based diet, you can leave out the meat, and the combination of grain corn and beans still contains all the amino acids your body needs to form proteins, making that combo a complete protein.

For most of our lives, we only grew green beans, the immature green pods of mature dry beans. Green beans make a great side dish, and we love roasting them up with olive oil and garlic or cooking them in tomato sauce for classic Syrian loubieh. But when it comes to filling your belly, mature dry beans and chickpeas blow green beans out of the water. There are few gardening activities we find quite as satisfying as picking a pile of brittle dry bean pods in the fall and cracking them open to reveal the gorgeous, colorful morsels of protein-filled goodness. Separating the dry pods from the beans is a meditative process, and it leaves you with bowls of sustenance deep enough to plunge your hands into.

Grocery stores sell dry beans cheaply, so from a financial perspective it might seem silly to grow them yourself. But growing staple crops packed with calories and protein, such as dry beans, can allow you to go for long periods of time without buying *anything* from the grocery store. Also,

Beans and corn together form a complete protein

homegrown dry beans are much more flavorful and sustainably grown than commercially produced dry beans, which are almost all grown in barren soil on monocropped megafarms and stored in warehouses for months or years where they lose some of their flavor before hitting store shelves. Dry beans are such a critical staple crop for us that our annual Living off the Land challenges usually begin when we finish harvesting them and end when we eat the last jar.

Seed Starting

Because of their equatorial heritage, beans like it warm. Wait until after your average last frost date to begin direct seeding or transplanting your beans outdoors. If you plant them too early, you risk the seeds rotting in the ground.

They tend to rot if planted too early because it's not yet warm enough for them to sprout, but it's plenty warm enough for fungal pathogens to begin consuming the dormant seeds. Once the soil warms enough for the seeds to sprout, though, the plant's immune system can keep fungal pathogens at bay.

Direct seeding works well for planting beans, but if you have poor germination, it can sometimes lead to patchy rows. To maximize our harvest and not leave open patches in our limited growing space, we usually start our seeds in 72-cell trays indoors and transplant them after the last frost. This method also gives them a bit of a head start that can help with pest and disease pressure later in the season. Starting them in trays and transplanting them is more labor-intensive, but we feel that it's worth it for the increase in yield.

Growing Conditions

Depending on the variety you're growing, you can use a few different methods for planting them in the garden. If you're growing a bush bean variety, like chickpeas, space them at 4 to 6 inches and plant them in a diamond pattern in your garden beds. If you're growing a vining variety, also called pole beans, they need a structure to climb on to maximize their production. This structure can be anything from trellis netting to a wooden lattice to sturdy cornstalks as detailed in the Companion Planting chapter (page 29).

If you're trellising pole beans, give them about 3 inches between plants and select a trellis that reaches at least 5 or 6 feet high. Once they take off, the plants will reach for the sky surprisingly fast. If you use cornstalks as your trellis, we recommend growing no more than two bean vines per cornstalk and using only sturdy grain corn varieties rather than sweet corn.

Jordan and his sister in their parents' bean tunnel

Pole beans find their trellises and grab hold well, but occasionally they start growing along the ground, in which case you need to train them onto the trellis initially. After that, they'll find their footing and grow like a weed. Growing up, Jordan and his sisters loved to crawl into the bean tunnel their mom, Heidi, grew over a low, arched trellis to harvest clusters of green beans hanging from the vines. If you have young kids, we highly recommend putting them in charge of a garden task like this to make them feel special and involved!

Beans require about 1 inch of water per week, either from rainfall or irrigation. If your soil is sandy or your region is extremely hot in the summer, you will likely need to water more frequently. Growing wide-leaved squash or pumpkins around the base of your bean vines in the traditional Three Sisters style helps prevent evaporation and keeps the soil cool and moist.

Beautiful legume flowers offer the first sign of your coming bean harvest. They can vary from purple, to pink, to mottled white. Beans self-pollinate, meaning they don't require insects or the wind to move pollen from their male to female parts. Shortly after the flower blooms, they will begin to form a pod. Once beans begin to grow, they grow *fast*. It usually only takes about a week to go from flower to pickable green bean.

You can pick any bean variety immature, as a green bean, or leave it to mature and harvest as a dry bean. Certain varieties of beans are bred to maximize the favorable characteristics of each type. Beans bred to be eaten green typically have more tender, "stringless" pods and smaller seeds. Beans bred to be eaten as mature dry beans often have tougher, stringy pods and larger seeds.

Pests and Diseases

The primary insect pest you might encounter on your bean plants is the Mexican bean beetle (*Epilachna varivestis*). These insects are closely related to ladybugs and are one of the few species in that family considered a garden pest rather than a garden helper. In their larval stage, they resemble plump yellow grubs and in their adult stage yellow ladybugs. Larvae and adults feed on bean leaves and pods, and they can be incredibly destructive in large numbers.

You can pick the grubs by hand and squish them, but if they're overwhelming your beans, we recommend treating them with pyrethrin. As we discussed in the Pest Management chapter (page 35), pyrethrin doesn't persist in the environment, but because it is toxic to many species of insect, you should still avoid spraying it when pollinating insects are active. Bean beetles overwinter in garden residue, so removing and composting your bean plants after the season finishes will help reduce their population for the following year.

When growing beans in heavy clay soils without adequate drainage, fungal diseases in the roots can become a problem. To avoid them, amend your soil with compost or other forms of organic matter. If you previously experienced fungal disease on your beans, avoid growing them in that area of the garden again for three to four years. Good crop rotation can help prevent the buildup of fungal and viral pathogens in the soil. If you live in an area with particularly high rainfall and humidity, fungal diseases can sometimes infect the leaves of your beans as well. To avoid or at least reduce this problem, plant your beans in an area of the garden with good airflow and space them a couple of inches farther than recommended previously to encourage the leaves to dry out between rainfall.

Bean beetle damage, a larva, and adult beetle

All that said, beans are generally a hands-off crop. You will likely have a great harvest regardless of the pressure from pests and diseases.

Our Favorite Varieties

We primarily grow a variety commonly called Cherokee Trail of Tears black beans, which is said to have been used as a subsistence crop by the Cherokee (Tsalagi) people to keep them from starving when the federal government forced them from their homelands in the late 1830s. This variety is excellent as both a green bean and a drying bean, and it consistently produces piles of delicious black beans for us every year. It also serves as an important reminder of where this ubiquitous crop comes from.

Good Mother Stallard beans are one of the most beautiful crops we grow, and we would probably grow them just to look at even if we didn't like to eat them. Luckily, they also taste delicious, so we regularly cook them in stews and soups. The plants seem to like slightly cooler conditions than the Cherokee beans, and this diversity helps us ensure a good harvest from one or the other variety, depending on the conditions from year to year.

Chickpeas are a bit of an unconventional garden crop in the United States, but hummus is a staple in our house, so we always dedicate a patch to these hardy legumes. Because of their long taproot, chickpeas can thrive in poor soils, so we plant them in the areas of our garden with the heaviest clay soil. During drought years, this soil can become so dry that the surface cracks, but the resilient chickpeas hold strong and still produce a crop.

Harvest and Preservation

We like to eat some fresh green beans during the summer, but to incorporate them in our meals all year long, we also process them for storage. The best way to preserve green beans is to blanch and freeze them because blanching destroys the enzymes that break down vegetables, cause discoloration, and rot them even in the freezer. Once blanched, green beans will freeze green and stay fresh all winter long.

Dry beans are one of the easiest crops to store and one of our favorites to process. You simply wait until the bean pods are dry and cracking on the plant, then collect them in a large bucket or even your shirt if you're unprepared. A lot

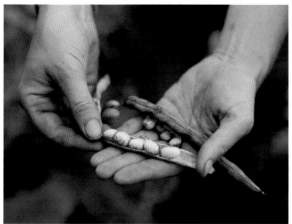

A Good Mother Stallard bean pod and beans

Hummus bi tahini (chickpeas with sesame paste)

of rain late in the season can sometimes lead to fungal disease, so if the dry beans are mature— soft yellowing or brown pods—but they aren't crunchy and dry yet, pick them early and finish drying them on a tray or screen indoors out of the rain.

The first year that our friends Melanie and Ethan grew a patch of dry beans, they stored their harvest in a glass jar and set it aside to use later in a winter stew. When December came, they opened the jar to discover that all the beans were hollow and the bottom of the jar was filled with a dry, sawdust-like substance. Unfortunately, the hollow beans and sawdust were the result of bean weevils (*Acanthoscelides obtectus*)

tunneling through the beans and eating them from the inside out. That's why it's always a good precaution to throw your jars of dry beans in the freezer for 24 to 48 hours before storing them. This destroys any bean weevil eggs lying in wait to gnaw through your harvest over the winter. After you remove them from the freezer, allow your beans to come to room temperature and dry out on the counter. After they turn bone-dry, free of any freezer condensation, jar the beans and store them at room temperature indefinitely. You can also heat your dry beans to 140°F in an oven or dehydrator for 15 minutes to eliminate any bean weevil eggs before storing them long-term.

A REALLY GOOD POT OF BEANS

It might sound boring, but a pot of beans—a *really good* pot of beans—is a life-changing dish. On its own, it's nourishing and satisfying, and it can form the basis of so many other meals. Using homegrown beans, spices, and aromatics from your garden results in something worlds apart from store-bought cans. When you let the beans take center stage, their personalities shine, and you can adapt your cooking to highlight their various attributes. White and beige beans, like the Good Mother Stallard and Hidatsa Shield Figure that we like to grow, taste nutty and creamy. Cherokee Black beans are firmer, so they work better in chilis and stews. Pinto beans' lower fiber content makes them perfect for blending into smooth, rich refried beans.

1 cup dry beans
1 tablespoon olive oil or butter
2 cloves garlic
1 smoked hot pepper
1 teaspoon ground cumin
1 teaspoon oregano
Salt

1. In a medium lidded pot, add the beans and 4 cups of water. Cover and soak them overnight.

2. In a large lidded pan over medium heat, heat the oil or melt the butter.

3. While the oil or butter is heating, mince or crush the garlic.

4. Add the garlic, hot pepper, cumin, and oregano and cook until fragrant, 1 to 2 minutes.

5. Add the beans and the soaking water and stir to combine.

6. Increase the heat to high and bring the water to a boil.

7. When the water boils, reduce the heat to low and cover the pan.

8. Simmer the beans until tender, adding water as needed to keep them submerged as they cook, about 45 minutes to 1 hour.

9. Salt to taste and serve.

LOUBIEH BI LAHME
[GREEN BEANS WITH MEAT]

Loubieh bi Lahme, a hearty Arabic stew that our family just calls Loubieh ("lew-bay"), makes an excellent comfort food for cold winter nights. It's one of our favorite ways to eat green beans, and it goes great with rice pilaf or a side of fresh Syrian bread. If you make it with meat, we recommend venison, lamb, or beef shank; for mushrooms, use the shiitake or oysters.

1 tablespoon olive oil

2 cups meat or mushrooms

3 cloves garlic

1 medium yellow onion

1 pound green beans

1½ teaspoons ground cumin

Salt

1 quart tomato sauce

1 cup water or broth of choice

1. In a large lidded pan over medium heat, heat the oil.

2. Add the meat or mushrooms and cook until browned nicely on all sides, about 5 minutes.

3. While the meat or mushrooms are cooking, crush or mince the garlic and chop the onion.

4. Add the green beans, garlic, and onion and stir to combine.

5. Add the cumin and salt to taste and cook until the onions become translucent and the garlic becomes aromatic, 5 minutes.

6. Add the tomato sauce and scrape loose any browned bits stuck to the bottom of the pan.

7. Add the water or broth to the sauce and bring the mixture to a boil.

8. When the sauce boils, reduce the heat to low, cover the pan, and simmer until the green beans become tender, about 1 hour.

9. Salt to taste and serve with rice pilaf or bread.

BEETS

Per Pound
CALORIES: 194   CARBS: 42.8 g   PROTEIN: 7.2 g   FAT: 0.8 g
IMPORTANT MICRONUTRIENTS: potassium

In North America, beets are a relatively uncommon food that occasionally make an appearance in roasted vegetables or a hearty soup, but many people unknowingly eat them every day in processed snacks. Beets are used to produce about 20 percent of the world's white sugar. The appropriately named sugar beets offer a great source of sweetness for folks growing food in a temperate environment where crops like sugarcane wouldn't survive the winter.

Beets were most likely first cultivated thousands of years ago by the Greeks and Romans. Early beets were primarily grown for their fleshy leaves, similar to what we now call "Swiss chard." Fun fact: Swiss chard is the exact same species (*Beta vulgaris*) as beets but bred for large leaves rather than large roots. The first recorded evidence of beets being grown for their bulbous roots was in the 1500s by farmers in what is now Germany and Italy.

Beets provide a great source of dietary fiber and carbohydrates. In our gardens, we grow a bed of beets each year to use in Venison Borscht (see page 74) and as a natural food coloring in wild red velvet cake. Silvan also likes to use them occasionally for blush and lipstick.

Seed Starting

You can seed beets directly in the garden or start them indoors in trays and transplant them when they are a few inches tall. Each beet seed is actually a little cluster of seeds fused together to form a dry fruit. Beets can be grown in clusters or "modules," which happens if you plant clusters without thinning them. For large round beets, thin them to one beet seedling every 3 inches. Many gardeners swear by the module-growing method, in which three or four beets grow together. In our experience, they often grow smaller this way but yield more beets per garden bed, so it's probably a similar yield either way.

Growing Conditions

Because they're very cold hardy, you can plant beets outdoors about six weeks before your average last frost and again in late summer for a winter crop. They can grow in partial sun, four to six hours per day, which will produce nice greens and a small root. If you want the quintessential big, round beetroots, plant them in full sun, six or more hours per day.

Beets are fairly short in stature and don't compete well with weeds, so stay vigilant and remove any unwanted plants that start shading them out in the garden. Spreading leaf mulch or grass clippings between your rows of beets can help prevent weeds from overtaking them and make your beet garden a little more hands-off.

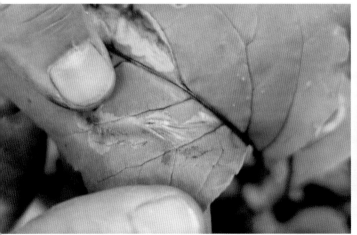

Leafminer damage on beet leaves

Pests and Diseases

The larvae of beet leafminers (*Pegomya spp.*) tunnel through beet and spinach leaves, destroying the cells as they go. You can identify these small grubs easily because of the conspicuous tunnels they leave in their wake. You can control them by squishing the larvae without tearing too much of the leaf. Several species of parasitic wasps and yellow jackets prey on them, so a beneficial insect habitat, such as a native wildflower garden, can help control them as well.

At the end of the season, remove and compost any potentially affected beet leaves from your garden because leafminer larvae overwinter in the residue and emerge as adults to lay eggs in your new crop in the spring. Disrupting this cycle won't eradicate them from your garden fully, but it will reduce their population significantly each year.

Our Favorite Varieties

For the classic red beet look and flavor, our favorite variety is Bull's Blood, which is named for its deep blood-red color. The Italian heirloom beet, Chioggia, features a beautiful pink striping and mild flavor for folks who aren't crazy about the classic earthy beet flavor. Touchstone Gold resembles orange carrots in color and tastes very sweet. Together these three varieties make a beautiful beet bouquet that can double as a decoration until you're ready to eat them!

Harvest and Preservation

When your beets reach your preferred size, simply pull them up, wash them, and they're ready for dinner. If you want to preserve them through the winter, lightly brush off any big chunks of soil rather than washing them, remove the leaves and taproot, and store them in a cool, dark place. Depending on the variety, they can keep in storage for months. Over the winter, we store ours in a wax-lined produce box in our garage, and last year we ate them well into the following spring.

PICKLED BEETS

Beets have a rich, earthy taste that works well with acidic flavors, so what better way to prepare them than pickling them in vinegar? We top sandwiches and tacos with these sliced pickled beets, and they make a great side with roasted venison or rich mushroom dishes.

2 cups vinegar

2 cups water

1 cup granulated white sugar

½ tablespoon salt

1 tablespoon coriander

1 tablespoon black peppercorns

5 pounds (10 large) beets

1. In a large pot over medium-high heat, combine the vinegar, water, sugar, salt, and spices and bring to a boil.

2. Meanwhile, wash the beets, removing any hidden soil. Slice them into ½-inch-thick slices.

3. Stuff the sliced beets into quart or pint jars.

4. When the salt and sugar have dissolved fully in the pickling liquid, pour it into the jars to cover the beets completely and seal the jars.

5. Let the jars cool to room temperature, then store them in the refrigerator.

VENISON BORSCHT

We initially approached borscht with skepticism, but it has become one of our favorite late-winter stews. Made with venison, borscht is a perfect dish for March in western Pennsylvania: hearty and satisfying to warm you on those blustery days spent preparing the garden for spring. If you don't have or want to use venison, skip it or substitute sturdy mushrooms, such as shiitakes. This soup tastes excellent as soon as it finishes cooking, but it's even better the next day, after the flavors have had a chance to mingle.

---

2 Tbsp olive oil

1 venison shank

1 or 2 cloves garlic

1 medium yellow onion

1 tablespoon tomato paste

2 tablespoons sherry

Vegetable or meat stock

3 or 4 large beets

3 or 4 medium potatoes

3 or 4 carrots

Salt

2 cups thinly sliced red or green cabbage

½ cup dill, plus more for garnish

1 or 2 tablespoons apple cider vinegar

Black pepper

Sour cream (optional)

1. In a large dutch oven or heavy pot over medium-high heat, add 1 Tbsp of the olive oil and brown the meat on all sides, about 5 minutes.

2. Meanwhile, dice the garlic and onions.

3. Reduce the heat to medium, add the garlic and onions, and cook until soft and translucent, about 5 minutes.

4. Add the tomato paste and stir to combine.

5. Add the sherry to deglaze the pan, then the stock, and bring the mixture to a boil.

6. When the sauce boils, reduce the heat to low and simmer until the meat becomes tender and pulls away from the bone easily, 1 to 2 hours.

7. Meanwhile, preheat the oven to 400°F and prepare the rest of the veggies.

8. Peel and chop the beets, potatoes, and carrots into pieces between ¼ and ½ inch thick.

9. In a large mixing bowl, toss the chopped veggies in the remaining tablespoon of olive oil and salt to taste.

10. On a baking sheet, spread the seasoned veggies in an even layer and roast them until tender, about 30 minutes.

11. When the meat slips easily from the bone, remove it from the pan, cut it into ½-inch-thick pieces, and return to the pan.

12. Add the roasted vegetables, sliced cabbage, and ½ cup of chopped dill.

13. Simmer until the cabbage becomes tender, 15 to 20 more minutes.

14. Add the vinegar and salt and pepper to taste.

15. Serve with a dollop of sour cream, if desired, and garnish with dill.

CABBAGE

Per Pound Raw
CALORIES: 112.5   **CARBS:** 26.1 g   **PROTEIN:** 5.8 g   **FAT:** 0.5 g
IMPORTANT MICRONUTRIENTS: vitamin C, calcium, potassium

Cabbage is one of the many cultivated versions of the species *Brassica oleracea*, which is commonly eaten all over the world. Kale, collard greens, and brussels sprouts are just a few of the many other iterations of this species. The original wild plant these crops were domesticated from is native to the eastern Mediterranean and western Asia, but the development of cabbage specifically is most often attributed to the Celts. The English word *cabbage* derives from the French *coboche*, which means "head," so the common phrase "head of cabbage" essentially means "head of head."

Cabbage has been a mainstay of European, Middle Eastern, and East Asian cuisines for centuries, forming the base of German sauerkraut, Arab stuffed cabbage rolls, and Korean kimchi. In the United States, store-bought cabbage often tastes fairly bland. Commercial cabbage varieties are bred for storage and shipping capabilities, not for flavor, and much of that cabbage grows in mild California weather. Like other brassicas, cabbage becomes sweeter and more flavorful after experiencing a cold spell in late fall. If you live in a temperate climate, you can make sure that happens by growing it yourself and allowing it to stay in the garden until winter.

We love to grow a little pile of dense cabbages to chop and ferment into sauerkraut, kimchi, and curtido every fall. The *Lactobacillus* bacteria do their work until they reach our desired level of funkiness, then we pack the dishes into quart jars and store them in the refrigerator, which halts fermentation. These jars can keep in the refrigerator for years, but we usually eat them all by the following spring. Sauerkraut tastes great with potatoes and slow-cooked venison, funky-spicy kimchi perfectly accompanies Korean scallion pancakes, and nothing goes better with corn and cheese pupusas than Salvadoran curtido.

Seed Starting

Give your cabbage a head start by starting it in seedling trays before transplanting it into your garden beds. We put two or three seeds in each cell of a seedling tray, then, after they sprout, remove all but the healthiest one.

After the seedlings have two true leaves and have grown about 2 or 3 inches tall, you can plant them in the garden. You can plant cold-hardy cabbage outdoors before the average last frost date, but it's best to harden them off for a few days first by taking them outside during the day and bringing them in at night. As a rule of thumb, start your seeds indoors about six to eight weeks before your average last frost date. If you plant

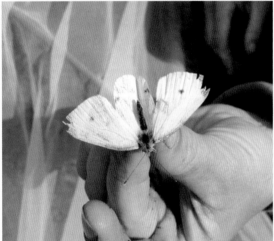

Cabbage looper larvae, cabbage white butterfly, and the damage they can cause

your cabbage in late summer for a fall or winter harvest, you can start your seeds in trays outside, but water them well to keep the summer heat from drying them out.

Growing Conditions

Depending on the size of the cabbage, space the plants anywhere from 12 to 24 inches apart. Compact varieties can grow closer together, large-headed varieties farther apart. Cabbage likes rich, well-draining soil, so we typically grow it in raised beds with a good amount of compost mixed in.

To form large dense heads, cabbage needs full sun (six or more hours per day). Any less than that and it will still grow, but it will be spindly and will likely not form a very dense head. Your cabbage should receive about 1 inch of water per week from rain or irrigation.

Pests and Diseases

As their names imply, cabbage is the target crop for cabbage loopers (*Trichoplusia ni*), cabbage whites (*Pieris rapae*), and cabbage aphids (*Brevicoryne brassicae*). Cabbage loopers and cabbage whites are both butterflies whose larvae feed on brassica leaves. The most effective way to stop them from harming your cabbage crop is to use floating row covers that prevent the butterflies from laying eggs on your plants in the first place. If you see just a few, you can pick them off by hand. If they're overwhelming your crop, spray them with Bt (the organic pesticide *Bacillus thuringiensis*).

Cabbage aphids generally pose more of a cosmetic problem, but if their population gets out of control, they can decrease the health of your plants by sucking sap and spreading plant diseases. To control the aphids, either physically spray them off the plants with a hard stream of water or spray them with insecticidal soap.

Rabbits, groundhogs, and other small mammals can cause major problems in a cabbage patch, but you can control them effectively with small chicken-wire fences or low tunnels with row covers.

Our Favorite Varieties

Caraflex is a short-season cabbage that is excellent for fresh eating. The green heads have a unique pointy shape, and the leaves are tender and sweet. For long storage, we grow a variety simply named "Storage #4 Green Cabbage." In cool storage, its large dense heads can last for more than a year! For red cabbages, we like to grow a small, quick-growing heirloom variety called Red Express.

Harvest and Preservation

Depending on the variety, your cabbage will be ready to harvest anywhere from 60 to 100 days after planting. Early-maturing varieties are generally smaller and are better for fresh eating, while later-maturing varieties typically have larger heads and a longer shelf life. When your cabbage starts to "head up," it will begin with a small, tight cluster in the center of the plant and expand outward. It's up to you when you want to harvest the head, but if it starts to open or crack, you may have let it grow a little too long, in which case you should harvest and use it right away.

In a refrigerator or root cellar, storage varieties can last for weeks or months, but the best way to preserve cabbage long-term is to look to the tool of our ancestors: fermentation. We love to learn new recipes for fermenting cabbage, and it seems like almost every culture has their own version!

CABBAGE SLAW WITH CARROT GINGER DRESSING

In the salad world, cabbage doesn't get as much love as lettuce or kale, but we more than make up for that. Cabbage stores so well that we end up eating a ton of slaws throughout the year, especially in the winter months, when fresh veggies are harder to come by. The crisp, juicy texture makes this dish simultaneously filling and refreshing, and its sturdiness allows it to stand up to bold dressings. We often make a bowl and eat it throughout the week as the perfect side dish for just about anything.

1 small head green cabbage

2 large carrots

3 radishes

½ cup Carrot Ginger Dressing (page 85)

¼ cup tahini

1 teaspoon whole-grain mustard

½ tablespoon honey

Juice of 1 lemon

1 tablespoon sesame or poppy seeds (optional)

1. Using a mandoline or box grater, shred the cabbage into fine pieces.

2. With a vegetable peeler, cut the carrots and radishes into thin strips or shred them on the box grater as well.

3. Place the shredded vegetables in a large bowl and mix well.

4. In a small mixing bowl, combine the Carrot Ginger Dressing, tahini, mustard, lemon juice, and honey. Taste and, if needed, adjust the seasoning or add water to thin the consistency.

5. Add the dressing to the slaw and toss to combine. If desired, top it with sesame or poppy seeds before serving for added texture.

SAUERKRAUT
[SOUR CABBAGE]

Pressure-canned and rendered sterile, supermarket jars of sauerkraut sit trapped in time, collecting dust. Alive and endlessly customizable when you make it yourself, homemade sauerkraut results from lactic acid fermentation by beneficial bacteria. At its most basic, sauerkraut consists of just cabbage and salt. In fact, the German word *sauerkraut* simply translates to "sour cabbage." Bacteria and time transform it into the sour, funky condiment we all know and love. We always make a few jars of the classic version, but we also mix it up with different spices and flavor combinations, adding garlic and hot peppers for a fiery sauerkraut perfect for tacos, or dill and horseradish for topping burgers. Consider the following more of a template than a recipe, and you'll be crafting your own special-edition sauerkrauts in no time.

---

1 medium cabbage
  (about 1 pound)
9 grams non-iodized salt (about
  1½ teaspoons)
Peppercorns, coriander seed,
  cumin seed, dill seed, and/
  or celery seed (no more than
  2 tablespoons total)

1. Core the cabbage and reserve a few large outer leaves for your fermentation vessel.

2. Finely shred the rest on a mandoline or with a sharp knife if you want a workout.

3. Weigh the shredded cabbage and write down the weight.

4. In a large mixing bowl, add the cabbage and 2 percent salt by weight (for example, 2 grams of salt for 100 grams of cabbage). Mix well and let sit for 10 minutes so the salt extracts the moisture from the cabbage.

5. Extract even more cabbage juice by crunching, pounding, and squeezing the shredded cabbage with your hands, or use a traditional wooden pounder. Either way, it's a lot of fun!

6. When a lot of juice has accumulated in the bowl, pack the sauerkraut into a fermentation vessel. For smaller batches, we use quart Mason jars. Pack it in layers tightly so that juice rises above the rest of the ingredients. Add any additional flavorings, such as garlic, shredded carrots, herbs, or spices.

7. Use one or two reserved cabbage leaves as a seal over your sauerkraut, pushing them down until the juice rises over them.

continued

8. On the cabbage leaf, add a weight of some sort: a sandwich bag filled with water, a purpose-made ceramic weight, or even a thoroughly cleaned rock.

9. Set your jars in a cool, unrefrigerated, dark place, such as a cupboard, and leave them for at least 1 week before testing. It should taste bubbly and tangy. A white film may coat the top. You can strain off this harmless yeast or mix it into the sauerkraut.

10. When the flavor and texture reach your liking, refrigerate the jar to slow fermentation. It will keep for several months.

CARROTS

Per Pound Raw
CALORIES: 184.5 **CARBS:** 43.1 g **PROTEIN:** 4.2 g **FAT:** 1.1 g
IMPORTANT MICRONUTRIENTS: vitamin A, potassium, beta-carotene, alpha-carotene, vitamin K

When Jordan was around 6 years old, his parents encouraged him to eat more carrots with his dinner. Their campaign started with a Bugs Bunny impression that involved taking a big bite of a carrot and saying, "Eh, what's up, Doc?" When the novelty wore off, they explained that carrots were good for your eyes and eating them can help you see better. Shortly after learning this information, he pulled a bag of carrots from the fridge, plopped down in a chair by the kitchen window, and ate every one of them, glancing out the window periodically to test his new supersight. The health effects of carrots are a little more subtle than young Jordan could understand, but they are an excellent vegetable to include in your diet and very easy to grow in the garden.

The first carrots were likely domesticated from a thin white root in central Asia just over 1,000 years ago, which makes them relative youngsters as far as domesticated vegetables go. According to historical records, early domesticated carrots were red, purple, and yellow. Over time, orange carrots came into fashion and even became the namesake for *carotenes*, the orange and yellow pigments in vegetables.

Modern carrots provide a wonderful source of vitamin A. It doesn't give you supersight, but vitamin A plays an important role in human vision. (Extreme deficiencies of it in children can even lead to blindness.) Carrots make a great raw snack when fresh and provide a unique, sweet flavor and texture to stews. Because they are relatively low in calories, we don't dedicate much space to carrots in our garden, but we always plant a couple beds because many of our favorite fresh salads and winter stews would be missing a critical element without them.

Seed Starting

Carrots have a long taproot, so, rather than starting them in trays and transplanting them, you need to direct-seed them in the garden. To direct-seed your carrots, use a stick or garden trowel to draw lines in the soil about ½ inch deep. Sprinkle in the seeds, aiming for 1 inch between each. If you plant them thicker than that, you can always pick some after they sprout, but that extra step makes for pretty tedious work. Sandy loam soil produces nice, long, straight carrots. Where we live, the soil is mostly Appalachian mountain clay, so we grow our carrots in raised beds with plenty of compost to loosen the soil.

Carrots can be very finicky in their initial germination or sprouting. This is especially true when they are planted in warm weather because the slightest bit of dry soil can delay germination. The best way to remedy this challenge is to cover the patch of seeded carrots with a sheet of soaking wet cardboard or a wet cloth. Lift the cardboard or cloth every few days, and as soon as you see any of the carrots breaking the soil surface, uncover them so they can access the sunlight. This process can take up to two weeks, and you might have to rewater the cardboard or cloth to prevent it from drying out before the carrots sprout.

Growing Conditions

Carrots are very cold hardy, so you can plant them in early spring for a summer harvest or in late summer for a fall or winter harvest. The bed needs access to full sun, so six or more hours per day, for them to develop a substantial root.

If you planted carrots in spring to harvest in early summer, harvest as soon as they reach your preferred size. If you leave them in the ground for too long in the summer, they can crack under the soil, especially with excessive moisture and heat. They are still edible if they crack, but the flavor and texture might not be optimal if they are a bit overgrown.

Alternatively, if you planted carrots in late summer for a fall or winter harvest, you can leave them in the ground through the winter and harvest them as needed. Carrots increase their sugar content to protect their cells from cold weather, so they will become sweeter as winter progresses.

Pests and Diseases

Carrots are generally very pest-free, but there are a couple of animals that can cause huge problems if they discover your garden. As many of us know from the previously mentioned childhood cartoons, rabbits love carrots. To keep them out, we recommend putting some kind of fencing around your entire garden. If that's not an option, surround at least your carrot patch with some kind of rabbit fencing or barrier. Groundhogs and other veggie-eating mammals can also become an issue, but rabbit fencing or chicken wire usually keeps them out as well.

Our Favorite Varieties

Our two favorite carrot varieties are Yaya and Danvers. Yaya carrots are very sweet and have a distinct carrot-y flavor. They are very tender and don't keep well, so we usually eat those soon after harvesting. Danvers are more substantial carrots and last longer in storage, so we save them for later in the season to use in soups and stews. If you're looking for a unique variety with a distinct flavor and color, we've heard good things about Cosmic Purple. Although we haven't grown them, they are said to have an almost spicy carrot flavor and a deep purple skin, which is a sign of powerful antioxidants called anthocyanins.

Harvest and Preservation

To store your carrots for winter, leave them in the ground and simply dig them up as needed. Cold weather stimulates them to produce sugar and ice-binding proteins, which act as a natural antifreeze and protect the roots in cold weather. If critters around the garden are looking for an easy winter meal, harvest your crop and store it in boxes in a basement or cool part of your house. You can simulate leaving them outside by packing them in buckets of cool, moist sand and leaving them in a garage or cold basement.

CARROT GINGER DRESSING

Here's our twist on the classic dressing you'll find at many Japanese restaurants. With so few ingredients, it's incredible how creamy and well-balanced it tastes. It adds a welcome brightness and tang to stir fries, roasted veggies, fish, and more. In the winter, we love making Cabbage Slaw (page 80) with it because it uses ingredients we always have in the pantry or freezer. If it's hard to grow or find baby ginger where you live, use mature ginger instead, but halve the amount and, since it's more fibrous, peel and chop it before adding to the blender. This dressing will keep well for several weeks in an airtight container in the fridge.

2 or 3 medium carrots

2 tablespoons fresh baby ginger

½ cup extra virgin olive oil

¼ cup rice vinegar

1 tablespoon honey

1 tablespoon soy sauce

1. Chop the carrots.

2. To a high-powered blender, add all ingredients and blend on high until smooth and creamy. If your blender has trouble grinding up the carrots, chop them smaller or add some water or a little more vinegar.

HONEY MUSTARD ROASTED CARROTS WITH THYME

Grated carrots with beets in a tangy mustard dressing make an excellent side for venison barbecue, but for making carrots the star of the show, you can't go wrong with simple oven roasting. A little honey or maple syrup provides a nice caramelization shortcut without having to cook the carrots so long that they dry out. This recipe uses thyme, but use whatever herbs or spices you like, such as coriander or cumin. This dish is delicious when served with yogurt and lemon juice. Sometimes, when we're living off the land, we soft-boil an egg, split it over a big pile of these carrots, and call it dinner.

1½ pounds (8 to 10) carrots

2 tablespoons olive oil

1 teaspoon salt

Thyme

Ground black pepper

1 tablespoon honey or maple syrup

1 tablespoon whole-grain Dijon mustard

1. Preheat the oven to 400°F and give the carrots a good scrub. We never peel ours, but if that's your preference, go for it. Keep slender carrots whole, cutting chunkier ones lengthwise into wedges. You want a lot of surface area for caramelization and crispiness while still retaining a tender middle.

2. On a baking sheet lined with parchment paper, spread the carrots in an even layer and drizzle with the oil. Sprinkle with the salt and thyme and black pepper to taste. Stir to coat evenly.

3. Roast them until they brown nicely on the outside and are fork tender, about 20 minutes.

4. Remove from the oven, keeping it on, and add the honey and mustard. Toss to coat and return the carrots to the oven until the honey mustard thickens into a sticky glaze, 4 or 5 more minutes.

5. Serve warm or let cool to room temperature.

CORN

Per Pound Dry
CALORIES: 1,642 **CARBS:** 334.4 g **PROTEIN:** 42.4 g **FAT:** 21.3 g
IMPORTANT MICRONUTRIENTS: magnesium, potassium, iron, and vitamin B
if nixtamalized

As we transitioned from growing vegetables that were profitable at the farmers' market, such as tomatoes and salad greens, and began to focus more on staple crops for nourishment, we knew grains would be a key piece of the puzzle. For many American, Middle Eastern, and European people, the first grain that comes to mind is probably wheat for making bread. Unfortunately, the space and labor required to produce a usable harvest of wheat aren't compatible with our small-scale, hand-powered style of gardening. Alternatively, flour corn was bred to have large easily harvested seed heads that you can process by hand. It also produces dense harvests in relatively small gardens. These properties have made corn the staple crop of choice in many Indigenous cultures throughout North America for thousands of years. Once we began to consider the meals of tortillas, cornbread, grits, tamales, and pupusas, it was a no-brainer to choose corn as the main staple crop for our gardens.

The story of corn began around 10,000 years ago in what is now southern Mexico with subsistence gardeners cultivating teosinte, a scrubby wild grass. Over generations, they selectively bred for larger and larger starch-filled kernels, eventually developing the ubiquitous grain that we now call corn or maize. The Spanish word *maiz* derives from the Taíno *mahiz*, which is how Spanish colonists first heard it described in the Caribbean Islands. The English word *corn* is simply the Old English word for "grain."

Although flour corn has a similar nutritional profile to whole wheat or rice when cooked and eaten whole, it has developed a pretty bad reputation in the United States because of its use as a sweetener in the processed form of high-fructose corn syrup. Many online "health experts" falsely claim that our bodies can't digest corn while simultaneously theorizing that corn is causing the obesity crisis. We'll leave it to them to explain how something you can't digest can make you gain weight.

But corn misinformation isn't new. About 500 years ago, it began when the Columbian Exchange introduced corn from Mesoamerica to Europe. Because it is easy to grow and yields calorie-dense harvests, corn quickly took hold as a staple food among the working class in Italy and Spain. Unfortunately, those two countries subsequently faced an epidemic of the debilitating disease pellagra. Over the next 200 years, doctors and scientists theorized that a toxin in corn had caused the outbreak of this new disease. But if that were the case, why did pellagra not afflict the peoples of the Americas who had eaten corn as their primary staple crop for 10,000 years? Through modern nutritional science, we learned that pellagra results from a vitamin B deficiency. From their conquests, Europeans had brought corn seeds back home but not the knowledge of how to process it properly.

The people of southern Mexico who first bred corn also developed the process of cooking it in an alkaline solution that breaks down the hull and unlocks vitamin B and other nutrients not bioavailable in raw corn. Today we call this process nixtamalization, from the Nahuatl words for "lime from ashes" and "corn dough," which describes the original method of creating the alkaline solution by using wood ashes to raise the pH of the water. Non-nixtamalized corn is a perfectly healthy staple crop when eaten with foods rich in vitamin B, including nuts, beans, or meat. On the other hand, if non-nixtamalized corn is solely making up the bulk of your diet—like it was for the Europeans experiencing pellagra—you should nixtamalize it to avoid missing that important vitamin.

Today, most nixtamalized corn is processed using the mineral calcium hydroxide, sold as *pickling lime* in the United States and Canada, and *cal* in Latin America. Nixtamalized corn is not only more nutritionally complete than raw corn, but its unique flavor and texture make it great for tortillas, corn chips, tamales, pupusas, and more. We cover how to nixtamalize your own corn in the Corn Tortilla recipe at the end of this chapter.

Despite some lingering misinformation, grain corn makes an excellent staple crop, and hundreds of millions of people around the world eat it daily. In our gardens, we dedicate significant amounts of space to flour corn and dent corn, where it grows alongside beans and squash, its

traditional sisters. If you live in North America and are working toward producing more of your own food, grain corn is practically a necessity in your garden.

Seed Starting

Large production farms always plant corn by direct seeding. This method can work fine in a small garden, too, but chipmunks, rats, squirrels, voles, and other critters love to eat it, which can pose challenges on a smaller scale. The first year we grew corn, we direct-seeded it, and rodents ate almost every kernel. When direct seeding corn, you also want to ensure that the soil is warm enough to germinate the seed quickly. If the soil is below 50°F, the seeds can take so long to sprout that fungal disease can consume them before they establish themselves.

As a solution to both problems, we start our corn seed indoors in seedling trays and transplant the seedlings into the gardens after our average last frost date. This method certainly requires more labor than direct seeding, but for us it's worth the effort. We even make an event of our annual corn-planting day. If you're growing corn on a larger scale, direct seeding after the soil temperature surpasses 50°F probably makes more sense. Just make sure to look out for hungry squirrels!

Growing Conditions

The two most common planting layouts for corn are conventional corn rows and traditional Three Sisters mounds. Across America, large growers use conventional rows to minimize labor, allowing easy access for tractors to apply fertilizer and herbicides and for massive combine harvesters to reap the corn at the end of the season. Traditional Three Sisters patches are the original method of growing corn that has been

A young Three Sisters patch

Corn silks leading to each kernel

used in North America for thousands of years. Because the mounds mix three plants that produce crops on different parts of the plant and they are harvested at different times, they are not ideal for mechanical harvesting and large-scale production. That said, they often produce more calories per square foot than conventional rows of corn and require fewer inputs, such as water and fertilizer.

If you do plan to grow conventional rows, space your plants about 6 to 8 inches within the rows and 2 to 3 feet between the rows. Maximize the number of rows to form as much of a square as possible, which will help with pollination later in the season. Even in conventional rows, you can plant climbing beans and winter squash at the base of the corn, which will give you a bonus harvest in the fall.

To grow Three Sisters mounds, pile soil in a circular mound, about 2 feet wide and 6 inches tall. Plant two to three corn plants per mound. Space the center of each mound 2 to 3 feet from its neighbors to provide room for vining squash to sprawl at the base.

Corn loves hot weather and full sun. When planning your garden layout, try to identify the sunniest part of the garden and dedicate that to your corn. Because corn is such a large leafy plant, it requires a good amount of water to develop well. Luckily, its roots can reach 6 feet deep at maturity, which allows it to access plenty of moisture. In our region in Pennsylvania, we typically receive enough rain that we don't need to water our corn much after the initial planting. In the dry Southwest, gardeners grow corn in almost desert-like conditions. Tyrell Descheny, a Navajo weaver and gardener, grows corn in the Southwest. We connected on social media through our mutual love of growing corn and being close to the land. Descheny plants corn in mounds spaced much farther apart than 2 to 3 feet and digs trenches between the mounds to allow occasional rain to pool at their bases. If too much time passes between rains, you can supplement the plants by filling the trenches with buckets of water.

As your corn establishes itself, weeds can easily overtake it. Before you know it, your corn

Silvan in a Three Sisters patch

patch barely resembles a garden. You can prevent this fate by cultivating or hoeing between the corn rows or mounds every other week until the corn reaches about 2 feet tall. At that point, it can outcompete the weeds. If you're using the Three Sisters method, the squash vines will begin sprawling and likely smother the weeds.

To a lot of folks, corn pollination remains a mystery, and new growers are often dismayed when they pick ears with a patchwork of missing kernels. The missing kernels are simply due to the fact that the kernel embryos were never fertilized by pollen. Corn plants produce pollen on the tassels at the top of the plant. This pollen blows down onto the silks that emerge from each ear. Every one of those silks corresponds to

Corn tassels and leaves

a kernel of corn, so any unpollinated silks end up as blanks on the cob.

If you have at least a 10-by-10-foot block of corn, the wind will naturally pollinate most of your ears. If you're growing a smaller plot than that, we recommend hand-pollinating to ensure good kernel production. This process is as simple as tapping the tassels to knock pollen onto the exposed silks in the morning. You can also collect pollen on a sheet of paper or in a paper bag and carry it around the garden to pollinate other silks.

Once your ears are pollinated, the waiting game begins. Depending on the variety, it takes about two months after pollination to form a mature ear of corn. Around pollination time, we fertilize our corn with high-nitrogen fertilizer, such as feather meal or fish emulsion, to give it a nutrient boost while it produces the ear. During this time, your ears of corn will go through a number of development stages, but the only ones you really need to know are the *milk stage* and *full maturity*. If you're growing sweet corn or want to harvest a few ears of flour corn early, harvest them during the milk stage, when the starches in the corn are still in a white liquid form and are most palatable fresh. For grain corns like flour, dent or popcorn, wait until full maturity to harvest the ears. It's easy to tell when an ear of grain corn has reached full maturity because the husk dries and turns brown, the kernels harden, and the cob will break away from the stalk when twisted.

Pests and Diseases

The primary insect pest that will impact your corn in most of North America is the corn earworm (*Helicoverpa zea*). These moths lay their eggs on the corn, and the larvae tunnel through the stalk or eat the fresh kernels as they develop. They often don't cause severe damage, so you

A corn earworm in action

Huitlacoche-infected corn

can simply cut off the damaged ends of the ears and eat the rest. As Silvan's grandmother used to say, "If the bugs don't want to eat it, why should I?" These moths typically overwinter in cornstalk residue, so an effective pest management strategy is to remove the stalks from your previous year's garden and compost them to keep the population in check.

Later in the season, damage from hungry rodents and deer can become an issue. If your garden doesn't have protection from mammals, consider harvesting your grain corn after it feels firm and the husks begin to dry but before it fully dries down. This strategy gives deer and rats less time to decimate your crop, and you can finish drying it by hanging it in your home, beyond the reach of critters. Winter squash vines are covered in tiny spines that contain an irritating, itchy substance, so they can also be an effective deterrent for small mammals—yet another benefit of the Three Sisters method.

The most common disease that impacts corn in the Americas is a fungus referred to as *corn smut* in the United States and *huitlacoche* in Mexico. Referring to it as a disease is actually a matter of perspective because it's a delicacy in parts of Mexico. Many people intentionally infect their cornfields to grow this delicious fungus. In our gardens, we wouldn't want our whole patch to be overtaken, but we don't mind finding a few ears exploding with the bulbous fungus, which we like to cook up in corn tortillas for quesadillas.

Our Favorite Varieties

Our favorite varieties of corn are Hopi Blue flour corn, Wapsie Valley dent corn, and Painted Mountain flour corn. Hopi Blue flour corn produces substantial ears of beautiful blue kernels. The soft starches make it excellent for nixtamalizing and grinding into masa to make soft blue tortillas or traditional Hopi piki. You can also pick Hopi Blue corn early and roast or steam it to eat like sweet corn.

Wapsie Valley dent corn is the workhorse of our sustenance gardens. It produces more calories than any other crop we grow, and it has a higher protein content than many other dent corns. The stocky plants easily hold multiple bean vines each and the hefty ears can produce nearly a pound of grain per cob. They also cook up into some of the most delicious grits and cornbread you will ever eat.

Painted Mountain flour corn is a short-season corn made from a cross of many differ-

Wapsie Valley corn

ent heirloom varieties, and the genetic diversity shows. Almost every ear looks completely unique, and the mesmerizing kernels run the gamut from pale blue to speckled dark red. Its soft starches make excellent tortillas, tamales, pupusas, and more.

Harvest and Preservation

If you're growing sweet corn, harvest it in the milk stage. You can tell that the corn is in the milk stage by peeling back the husk and pressing your fingernail into a kernel. If a milky liquid bursts out, it's ready to harvest.

We grow most of our corn for grain, so we typically wait for full maturity to harvest. When the ears begin to dry on the stalk and hang heavy, they're ready to pick. At this stage, the only remaining task is to tie them up and hang them to ensure they are fully dried down, at which point they will store at room temperature indefinitely. We leave a few layers of husk on each ear to tie them in bunches, which we hang from our living room ceiling and in a sunny spot on our porch.

If you're growing a popping corn, moisture levels are critical for good popping. First-time popcorn growers commonly don't let their popcorn dry down enough, so when they throw it in the pan to pop, it simply burns. We don't have any equipment that a professional popcorn grower would use to measure moisture content, so we hang it up to dry and every once in a while we throw a few kernels in a hot pan. When they all pop, we remove the kernels from the cobs and store them in jars to retain that moisture level.

We eat most of our corn as grits, cornmeal, and nixtamal. Cornmeal is actually a by-product of making corn grits, or maybe it's the other way

around, depending on your perspective. Either way, they are produced together. To make cornmeal and grits, we use a hand-powered stone grain mill to grind our dried corn, then a fine mesh sifter to separate the coarser grits from the fine cornmeal.

Nixtamal is corn that has been processed using an alkaline solution to break down the hull and unlock some vitamins that are not bioavailable in raw corn. It's also called hominy. Read the Corn Tortillas recipe that follows for details on how to nixtamalize your corn.

CORN TORTILLAS

Making tacos with homegrown corn tortillas is incredibly rewarding. We love tacos filled with slow-cooked venison, thinly sliced radishes, and pico de gallo. When we want a crunchy snack, we cut some tortillas into wedges and fry them up for chips.

Grain corn
Pickling lime (cal)
Salt

1. Weigh the corn and write down the weight.

2. Calculate 1 percent of the corn weight and weigh out that amount of pickling lime.

3. In a large lidded pot, add the corn, cover it with water, and bring the water to a boil.

4. Cook for 5 minutes, then stir in the pickling lime.

5. Reduce the heat to medium-low and simmer the corn until soft enough for a fork to crush it, about 1 hour. Add water as needed to keep the corn submerged.

6. Turn off the heat, cover the pot, and let it sit overnight.

7. Pour the corn through a colander and rinse off the pickling lime solution.

8. Using a hand mill or high-powered food processor, grind the corn into dough (masa).

9. Salt to taste.

10. Roll the masa into 1-inch-diameter balls.

11. Form the tortillas with a tortilla press or two large plates or books lined with a clean plastic bag or wax paper.

12. On a smoking hot pan or comal, cook the tortillas about 1 minute per side. Flip them once the edges begin to curl.

13. Eat them fresh or place them between paper towels in a plastic bag and freeze them for later.

continued

JALAPEÑO CORN BREAD

This go-to winter staple makes an excellent accompaniment to venison stew (Lou-bieh bi Lahme, page 69), Collard Greens and Beans (page 112), and more! After grinding the corn, all you need to do is mix the ingredients in a bowl and pour them into a hot pan. It's one of the simplest recipes in this book.

2 cups cornmeal

1 tablespoon shredded deer tallow or frozen butter

1 teaspoon baking powder

1 teaspoon baking soda

1 teaspoon salt

2 large eggs

1 jalapeño or serrano pepper

1 cup water

½ cup cooked pumpkin purée

1 tablespoon high-heat oil, such as peanut

1. Preheat the oven to 375°F.

2. In a small mixing bowl, combine the dry ingredients.

3. In another small mixing bowl, beat the eggs with a splash of water.

4. Mince the pepper and add it to the eggs.

5. Add the remaining wet ingredients to the egg mixture.

6. While stirring with a fork, add the wet ingredients to the dry ingredients.

7. In an oven-safe skillet over high heat, spread the oil and pour in the cornbread batter. Cook for 4 minutes for a crispy crust.

8. Transfer the skillet to the oven and cook until the top of the cornbread browns, about 25 minutes.

GARLIC

Per Pound
CALORIES: 670   CARBS: 148.9 g   PROTEIN: 28.6 g   FAT: 2.3 g
IMPORTANT MICRONUTRIENTS: calcium, potassium, zinc, vitamin C

Silvan has loved garlic for a long time. For her birthday as a young child, she received a cloth pig puppet, which she named Garlic. Not content with her new friend merely suggesting an association with one of her favorite flavors, she stuffed a clove of raw garlic in the pouch of her new toy. From then on, Garlic the Pig reeked of his namesake, and if his garlicky odor ever faltered, she replaced the garlic clove with a fresh one. Her parents allowed and even encouraged this strange behavior. Maybe they knew an obsession with garlic has been part of human history for centuries.

Few food plants are as storied and controversial as garlic. Its origins as a cultivated crop are debated, but there is evidence of garlic being grown by people in Egypt and India as early as 5,000 years ago. Its reputation has had many ups and downs. In ancient China, people highly regarded it as an aphrodisiac and potent medicine, while in ancient Greece, temple sentinels turned away would-be worshippers with even a hint of garlic on their breath. Whether loved or disdained, garlic has always had power. Some people consumed it to increase strength and stamina, and some to ward off vampires, evil, and sickness. Others sealed it into tombs with the pharaohs for the afterlife.

Garlic's power and pungency come from allicin, a sulfuric compound that performs a bit of a magic trick. Whole cloves have relatively little odor, but chop one up or chew it, and its fiery aroma and flavor leap into action. When exposed to air, the sulfurous molecules in the garlic react, transforming into new compounds with strong antimicrobial and anti-inflammatory properties. In the kitchen, we use this interesting bit of chemistry to change the flavor of garlic in our meals. Garlic that is put whole into bubbling oil or broth will have little of the kick of raw garlic, staying mild and sweet. On the other hand, crushing a clove and letting it sit for 15 minutes before adding it at the end of cooking will give any dish the full effect of those sulfur compounds.

We love growing and eating garlic. In our house, almost every meal starts with pulling a clove from one of the bundles dangling from our dining room wall. We could grow twice as much as we currently do and have no problem using it all. As a crop, it's incredibly easy and low-maintenance, and in our northern climate it has the rare distinction of being a crop planted in the late fall for harvest the following summer. Tucking the tiny cloves into the soil as the cold winter settles in around us is a wonderful act of hope for the year to come.

Seed Starting

Garlic comes in two major categories: hardneck and softneck. If you see something called *elephant garlic* in seed catalogs, it has a much milder flavor, and technically it's a leek. Hardneck garlic has a (surprise) hard neck, and it sends up a

flower stalk, also called a scape. Grocery stores commonly sell softneck garlic. It has large bulbs with many cloves and stores for a very long time. Because it doesn't send up a seed stalk, the stem remains soft and flexible and, after harvest, you can braid it easily for storage. Hardneck garlic resembles garlic's wild ancestors, and as such has a greater variety of shapes, colors, and flavors, making it a beloved staple of home gardens. Hardneck garlic cloves are generally very large in size but fewer in number, and they don't last as long in storage as softneck varieties.

Similar to potatoes, garlic is typically grown from clones of the cloves themselves rather than seed. Somewhat confusingly, these cloves are referred to as *seed garlic*. You can grow garlic from the grocery store, but we recommend buying certified disease-free organic seed garlic from reputable suppliers. These sellers test

the bulbs for common garlic ailments and produce them specifically to grow well in organic gardens. They also offer a fun array of different varieties to choose from. You can usually begin buying seed garlic online or at local garden supply stores in late summer. Gourmet garlic is one of the few gardening items where demand consistently seems to outstrip supply. (Here's your sign to start a seed garlic farm!) Seed garlic regularly sells out, especially from specialty suppliers with the biggest variety, so don't wait too late to place your order. After buying an initial supply of seed garlic, you can usually save cloves from your own harvests to replant year after year, purchasing more stock only when you want to try a new variety.

Planting garlic is usually our last big garden task of the year, a fun way to end the growing season with an investment in the future. In most of North America, September through November is the best time to plant garlic. Plant it after the first fall frost but about a month before it gets really cold and the ground freezes. This scheduling gives the cloves enough time to send out roots but not too much time in warm soil, which can cause them to rot or send up leaves that will die back once the weather turns. Plant your cloves 2 to 4 inches deep in rich, well-draining soil. Space the plants anywhere from 6 to 12 inches apart, depending on the size of the variety. Planting your cloves farther apart will generally result in bigger heads of garlic, but some people prefer more numerous, smaller ones instead. Plant the cloves with the root end downward and the pointy tip toward the sky.

After planting, we mulch our garlic with a thick layer of straw or leaves, which helps protect it from major cold snaps and doubles as weed protection the following spring. At the time of planting, we usually add some balanced organic

Chicken manure can boost your garlic.

fertilizer. This slow-release amendment becomes available to the cloves when they start growing in earnest the next year. Adding composted manure on top of your beds works similarly. At Silvan's workplace, she always adds composted chicken manure from their laying hens to the garlic beds, which results in nice big bulbs.

Growing Conditions

After tucking in your garlic for the winter, it's basically hands-off until the following spring. As the soil warms, the thick green leaves will emerge from the mulch. Leave the mulch in place unless you live in a very northern climate and need the soil to warm quickly. Garlic, like all alliums, doesn't compete well with weeds at all, and your yield will suffer dramatically if you let weeds infiltrate your garlic beds. Mulching keeps the weeds at bay in the most hands-off method, and you don't have to worry about your garlic bed until harvest time.

In warmer climates, growing big garlic can be challenging due to the mild winters and hot summers. Garlic, especially the hardneck varieties, requires a lengthy period of cold weather to begin growing bulbs at the right time. If temperatures in your area don't fall consistently below freezing in wintertime, you can "trick" your garlic. Refrigerating your garlic seed bulbs for several weeks before planting, a process called vernalization, can give them the jolt of cold they need to make big bulbs the following year. If your soil warms quickly in spring, heavily mulching your garlic beds with straw, leaves, or wood chips will keep it cooler longer and prevent your garlic from bulbing too soon, which will result in smaller bulbs. Light-colored mulches reflect more sunlight and keep the roots cooler than dark mulches or bare soil. In very warm, sunny climates, adding shade cloth over your garlic beds to protect them from the harshest rays can help as well.

In mid to late spring, hardneck garlic sends out flower stalks or scapes. Harvest the scapes soon after they emerge because as they develop they pull energy from the roots, resulting in smaller bulbs. When growing hardneck garlic, scapes make a delightful bonus crop, with a crisp texture and mild, garlicky flavor. We like to pickle them, ferment them, or throw them in batches of pesto.

Pests and Diseases

Garlic is generally an easy, low-maintenance plant in the home garden, but there are a few problems to watch out for. Soil-borne diseases can damage garlic. To protect against them, buy certified disease-free seed garlic when planting for the first time. When selecting seed garlic from your own harvest to plant the following year, choose healthy, disease-free plants. During the growing season, remove any diseased-looking plants as soon as symptoms develop to prevent diseases from spreading to the rest of the crop. Signs of disease include browning and wilting leaves early in the season, dark lesions or spots on the stem, and rot or mold where the garlic stem meets the soil.

Fusarium rot, a particularly gnarly family of garlic diseases, creates brown lesions all over the bulbs, leaving them shriveled and inedible. The fusarium fungus responsible for these diseases exists in almost all soil, so preventing it from becoming a problem is a matter of good growing practices like rotating your garlic planting areas when needed and immediately removing any garlic showing symptoms.

Because of its pungency, garlic tends not to attract big pests like groundhogs or deer. Some smaller pests happily dine on garlic bulbs, however. Wireworms, the larval stage of click beetles (*Ctenicera spp., Agriotes sputator*), frequently tunnel into garlic bulbs, leaving little holes all over the surface. In most cases, these are simply a nuisance rather than a danger to the plant, but extreme wireworm infestation can damage the bulbs enough to kill the plants or create avenues for diseases to strike. It's unlikely, but if you have a high wireworm population in your soil, a cover crop of mustards can help suppress them.

Our Favorite Varieties

After buying plain white garlic from the grocery store for so long, perusing the huge selection of varieties to grow in the garden can feel fun and potentially overwhelming. Search for garlic seed farms in your growing zone and follow their recommendation for varieties that thrive in your particular climate. Over time, saving and replanting healthy garlic from your harvests will adapt them to your garden's specific conditions.

Here in zone 6b in western Pennsylvania, we frequently grow German White, a hardy and reliable variety, as well as Music, known for its jumbo bulbs. Chesnok Red, a beautiful hardneck variety, has reddish-purple striping, and it performs well in both northern and southern states. Georgian Crystal, a hardneck variety known for its huge bulb size, grows well even in warm southern climates. For very warm locations, your best bet is a softneck variety like Silverwhite, which is one of the longest-storing varieties.

Harvest and Preservation

Your garlic will usually be ready to harvest in early summer. As the bulbs mature, the outer leaves will begin to get dry and become brittle. At this stage, we pull test plants every week to check for maturity. The garlic bulbs are ready when you can feel firm, individual cloves and the outer skin feels thick but papery. If you're irrigating your garlic, stop watering it a week or two before you plan to harvest. If any of your bulbs are splitting open to reveal the cloves within, harvest the rest of your garlic very soon. Open bulbs are fine to eat, but they don't last as long in storage.

When harvesting, use a pitchfork on the outer edges of the bed to avoid slicing through your precious garlic bulbs. Your goal here is just to loosen the soil so you can pull the garlic plants without damaging the bulbs or necks. If it has rained recently or you have particularly loose soil, you may not even need the pitchfork. Handle your garlic gently at this stage because it hasn't cured yet and is susceptible to bruising and scratching that will undermine its shelf life.

After harvesting your garlic, clean it and cure it. Depending on your soil, a lot of clay and dirt may be clinging to your bulbs. Carefully scrape or brush it off, leaving the bulbs attached to the stalk. You can peel off an outer leaf or two to reveal the clean skin below, but leave a couple layers of skin on your bulbs; they will form the papery protective husk to keep the cloves fresh in storage.

Put your garlic plants somewhere with lots of ventilation but no direct sunlight or precipitation. We usually tie ours in bundles of 10 to 15 plants and hang them from nails on our covered

A hanging garlic braid

porch. Another great option is to lay your garlic plants out on a shelf fitted with mesh racks. If you need to cure your garlic indoors, use a box fan in the space to move air around and over the garlic. After several weeks, the leafy tops will have dried completely and turned a brownish yellow. If you pinch the "neck," where the stem meets the top of the bulb, it should feel dry and hollow rather than squishy. At this point, you can cut the tops off your garlic. We usually trim off the roots at this point, too, since they have become brittle and easy to cut. Inspect your bulbs for damaged cloves and eat those bulbs first. Discard any bulbs with mold or obvious disease.

After the bulbs cure, store your garlic in a cool, dry place away from direct sunlight. If properly cured and stored, garlic bulbs should last until the next garlic planting season—assuming you don't eat them all first!

TOUM

Toum means "garlic" in Arabic, and that's pretty much all this sauce is. The lemon juice and oil cut through the intensity of the raw garlic, but toum still packs a serious garlic punch! This dipping sauce works perfectly with the bold flavors of steak, grilled mushrooms, or falafel.

10 to 12 medium cloves garlic
1 small lemon
1 teaspoon salt
1½ to 2 cups neutral oil

1. Peel the garlic cloves and add them to a food processor.

2. Juice the lemon for 2 tablespoons of fresh juice.

3. Add the salt and lemon juice to the food processor and pulse to mince the garlic.

4. Slowly add the oil in a thin stream while running the food processor on high speed.

5. As soon as the mixture begins to emulsify or form a homogenous paste, stop adding oil.

6. If the mixture doesn't emulsify fully, add a splash of cold water and run the food processor until the sauce becomes smooth.

ROASTED GARLIC SOURDOUGH BREAD

There's nothing wrong with buttered toast sprinkled with garlic powder, but if that's your only experience with garlic bread, you're in for a treat. The whole roasted garlic cloves smashed into crusty bread with a drizzle of olive oil can make a meal all on its own, but it also goes great with pasta, soup, or a big salad.

12 cloves garlic

6 slices sourdough bread

1 tablespoon olive oil

Salt

1. Preheat the oven to 350°F.

2. On an unlined baking sheet, roast the whole cloves of unpeeled garlic until they feel soft when squeezed, 30 to 40 minutes.

3. Remove them from the oven and let them cool for 10 minutes.

4. Meanwhile, toast the bread.

5. When the roasted cloves are cool enough to handle, squeeze the soft roasted garlic from the papery husks onto the bread. Spread it with a knife to coat the bread evenly.

6. Drizzle olive oil over the garlic toast and sprinkle with salt to taste.

KALE AND COLLARDS

Per Pound
CALORIES: 144 **CARBS:** 24.4 g **PROTEIN:** 13.6 g **FAT:** 2.7 g
IMPORTANT MICRONUTRIENTS: calcium, magnesium, iron, potassium, vitamin C, folate, vitamin A, vitamin K

Collards and kale are just two of the many examples of the incredible diversity of one species of plant: *Brassica oleracea*. Their wild ancestor, a weedy cabbage, likely originated in the eastern Mediterranean and western Asia, but people have cultivated it for so long that its exact origin is unknown. Cabbage, broccoli, cauliflower, brussels sprouts, and kohlrabi all arose from this same ancestor, making *Brassica oleracea* an amazing case study in the power of our ancestors' classical plant breeding.

Throughout the centuries, kale and collards have gone in and out of fashion, which probably says more about humans' tendency to create trends around food than the innate qualities of these two stalwart greens. For centuries, kale was grown in the gardens of the Roman Empire, then the English relegated it to cattle feed or peasant food, considering it fit only for people who couldn't afford anything else. In the United States, collards were commonly eaten by enslaved Africans in the South, who drew on the West African tradition of making hearty stews of long-cooked greens seasoned with a small amount of meat. Despite collards being rich in vitamins and minerals and one of the easiest greens to grow year-round, their association with slavery gave them a reputation for being an unhealthy food for people living in poverty.

In North Carolina, collard greens were a regular staple of Silvan's family. Cooked in oil and seasoned with salt and vinegar, the thick, hearty leaves are the classic accompaniment to hush puppies and North Carolina–style barbecue. In our household, we eat collards regularly and find them to be the perfect way to fill our bellies and cut through the richness of corn grits and venison barbecue.

Seed Starting

Like other brassica crops, kale and collards benefit from being started indoors in early spring to get a head start on the season. We start our seeds in 72-cell trays or small pots, putting two seeds in each hole and then only keeping the healthiest one if they both sprout.

When the seedlings have two or three true leaves, we harden them off—setting them outside and bringing them back in at night for a few days—then plant them in the garden. This process acclimates them to outdoor temperatures and prepares them for cold early spring nights.

For a spring crop, we typically start our kale and collards about six to eight weeks before our average last frost date. If you plant your kale and

Collard leaves

collards in the summer for a fall harvest, start them outdoors in seedling trays in the late summer as soon as the harshest heat starts to give way to cooler fall breezes.

Growing Conditions

Kale and collards do well in most garden conditions as long as they receive adequate water. Their leaves will grow more substantially in full sun, six or more hours per day, but they can get by with partial sun, four to six hours per day. Space the plants about 8 to 12 inches apart to avoid too much competition between plants. You can grow kale a little closer together and harvest the leaves, when small and tender, for a salad crop.

Keep them well-weeded while still small.

Once they establish a large canopy of leaves, they'll shade out the soil beneath them and prevent most weeds from germinating. We often take advantage of the time it takes for the canopy to grow in by planting a quick-growing crop, such as lettuce, scallions, or radishes, between our kale and collards and harvesting that crop before the bed gets too crowded.

Here in zone 6b, we can start kale and collards in early spring and, if temperatures don't dip too low, harvest from the same plants through fall and even winter. In hotter climates, it's better to grow them from fall through spring, taking a break in summer, when the heat stresses the plants and makes the leaves tough or causes them to go to seed. As with cabbage, frosts cause kale and collards to convert starches in their leaves into sugars as a kind of natural antifreeze, making them extra sweet and tender. Winter-harvested kale and collards will be some of the best greens you've ever tasted. We occasionally eat them raw, right off the plant, in the snow.

Pests and Diseases

The larvae of cabbage loopers (*Trichoplusia ni*) and cabbage whites (*Pieris rapae*), both butterflies, feed on brassica leaves. You can prevent them from harming your crops by using floating row covers that prevent the butterflies from laying their eggs on your plants in the first place. They can also be picked off by hand if the infestation is light. If you find that your kale and collards are constantly covered in holes and handpicking the pests isn't cutting it, we recommend spraying your crop with Bt, the organic pesticide *Bacillus thuringiensis*.

Rabbits, groundhogs, and other small mammals love to eat kale and collards. If you don't have a good fence around your garden, a temporary low tunnel topped with row cover can disguise and protect your plants from would-be diners. Be sure to pin it down securely at the base with stones or other heavy objects because groundhogs are especially adept at finding weaknesses and holes in garden defenses!

In a home garden, when part of a diverse planting, kale and collards don't have a lot of disease pressure. Warm, humid weather can occasionally cause bacterial or fungal problems, however. Black rot, a bacterial disease that causes yellow and black lesions on leaves that eventually rot the heads of the plants, can devastate yields. As a good preventive practice, maintain adequate air flow by giving plants enough space and removing old, dying leaves. Immediately remove any leaves with signs of disease because the disease can spread to other leaves through water droplets. If any of your brassicas develop black rot, consider moving them to a different area of your garden for at least three years to let bacteria levels subside.

Our Favorite Varieties

One of our favorite kale varieties to grow is lacinato—also called Tuscan kale, dino kale, or *cavalo nero*. Lacinato is an extremely winter-hardy variety and makes a great base for a massaged kale salad. Green curly kale varieties, such as Curled Blue Scotch, can withstand cold and hot weather, making them good all-purpose cultivars. Red Russian kale is a particularly tasty and tender variety that thrives in cool weather but not in the summer. The aptly named Champion collards are the only variety of collard greens we grow. Their huge, thick leaves handle hot weather with ease, and they can survive Pittsburgh winters uncovered and fully exposed to the elements.

Harvest and Preservation

You can eat kale and collards fresh, in a hearty salad, or cook them with oil for sautéed greens. If you plan to eat them fresh, use them within a week of harvest to avoid wilting and yellowing. If you're going to cook your greens later in the season, blanch them in hot water and freeze them for long-term storage. We blanch big piles of greens and divide them into baseball-sized portions that we freeze individually and then bag. Throughout the winter, whenever we want to cook up some greens, we just pull out a chunk and defrost it.

KALE SALAD

This is one of the few dishes we can have year-round because kale is such a garden superstar. We eat some variation of this recipe about once a week. Toppings can vary, even the brassica itself, but the foundation remains the same: cutting it into small strips; massaging it so it becomes tender yet still crunchy; and topping it with a tangy, garlicky dressing. In spring and summer, we love it with hard-boiled eggs and roasted new potatoes. In winter, it becomes a perfect meal with some venison steaks on top.

FOR THE DRESSING

1 lemon
¼ cup olive oil
2 tablespoons Dijon mustard
2 tablespoons tahini
1 teaspoon salt
1 teaspoon ground black pepper
¼ cup grated Parmesan cheese (optional)

FOR THE SALAD

1 large bunch lacinato kale
2 medium carrots
3 or 4 radishes, sliced
2 or 3 salad turnips

1. First, make the dressing. In a large mixing bowl, juice the lemon for 2 tablespoons of fresh juice.

2. Add the rest of the dressing ingredients and stir to combine.

3. If using fresh kale, wash and dry it. Separate the leaves from the ribs. Discard the ribs and chop the leaves into ribbons.

4. Add the kale ribbons to the dressing and massage them gently for at least 1 minute.

5. Slice the carrots with a vegetable peeler, chop the radishes and turnips, and add them to the kale. Toss to combine.

COLLARD GREENS AND BEANS

This is our twist on an Italian classic and one of Silvan's favorite vegetarian meals. This one-pot meal makes a great weeknight dinner, and dry beans from the garden generally cook much faster than store-bought, so you can skip the soaking. Customize your greens and beans with different herbs and seasonings, depending on the time of year. In summer, we often add basil or a dollop of pesto; in wintertime, warming herbs, such as rosemary.

1 cup dried cannellini, Good Mother Stallard, or other soup bean

3 tablespoons olive oil, divided

2 stalks celery

1 small yellow onion

3 or 4 cloves garlic

1 teaspoon dried chili flakes

2 cups vegetable stock or water

Parmesan cheese rind

Salt

1 bunch (½ pound) collard greens

1 lemon

Freshly ground black pepper

1 cup grated Parmesan cheese

1. In a medium lidded pot, add the beans and 4 cups of water. Cover and soak them for 12 hours. If using fresh beans, skip this step.

2. In a large pot over medium heat, heat 2 tablespoons of olive oil.

3. Mince the celery and onion and cook until both become soft and translucent, about 5 minutes.

4. Meanwhile, rinse the beans and slice the garlic.

5. Add the chili flakes and garlic and cook until fragrant and the garlic just turns brown, about 1 minute.

6. Add the beans, vegetable stock, and Parmesan rind, increase the heat to medium-high, and bring to a boil.

7. Reduce the heat to medium-low and simmer, stirring occasionally, until the beans become tender. Timing can vary widely based on the variety and freshness of the beans. Test their texture after 30 minutes. Salt to taste.

8. Strip the leaves from the collard greens and chop them into pieces about ½ inch wide. Add the chopped greens to the pot, stirring to combine and wilt them, and cook until tender, 5 to 10 minutes.

9. Meanwhile, zest the lemon into a small bowl, then juice it.

10. Add the lemon juice, freshly cracked pepper, and the remaining tablespoon of olive oil.

11. Ladle into serving bowls and sprinkle each with Parmesan cheese and lemon zest. Serve with crusty bread.

MICROGREENS

Per Pound
CALORIES: 162   **CARBS:** 21.2 g   **PROTEIN:** 21.2 g   **FAT:** 0 g
IMPORTANT MICRONUTRIENTS: calcium, potassium
Details will vary based on the type of microgreens.

Unlike the other vegetable crops in this book, microgreens aren't a specific type of plant but the stage at which you harvest an array of different plants. In fact, if you have excess seeds, you can grow and harvest many of the other crops in this book as microgreens.

The word *microgreens* makes us think of an overpriced restaurant with tiny, artfully arranged portions and entrées like lobster foam and pancake bubbles. We've never eaten at that kind of restaurant—and we're pretty sure we just made up "pancake bubbles"—but we eat microgreens regularly.

In stark contrast to their reputation as a high-end extravagance, microgreens are dirt cheap to produce and make excellent use of old seeds that otherwise might go to waste. In winter we grow microgreens in seedling trays, which allows us to eat fresh produce when snow blankets the dormant outdoor garden.

Seed Starting

Our go-to method of growing microgreens is to spread a 1-inch layer of moist potting soil in a 10-by-20-inch seedling tray and liberally seed the surface. We lightly press the seeds down to

increase soil-to-seed contact, which helps with germination, especially for older seeds.

To prepare your potting soil, add water until it holds together when squeezed but isn't dripping. If it drips when squeezed, it's too wet. The amount of seed to use varies greatly depending on seed size. You can space microgreens more tightly than other seedlings because you harvest them so small, but you should still provide a little space between seeds so they don't compete for soil and light. We spread them so each square inch of potting soil has about five to 10 seeds, but if you find yourself counting out seeds for each square, you're being *way* too careful. Our technique is to grab a handful and sprinkle them from about a 12-inch height, which will spread them out nicely.

Growing Conditions

To increase your germination rate, cover your tray with a wet towel and place it in the warmest spot in your home until the seeds sprout. We sit ours on a radiator. After a few days, the seeds will sprout. Immediately move the tray under a grow light or into your sunniest window.

Keep a spray bottle on hand and check for dryness once or twice per day. Your microgreens shouldn't be dripping with water constantly, but the soil needs to stay moist at all times. The time from seeding your tray to harvest can be as short as a week, so if you're used to nurturing tomatoes for months before tasting their fruit, this harvest will seem like it came in the blink of an eye!

Pests and Diseases

Microgreens are pretty much pest-free, especially if grown indoors. The one issue that can sometimes arise is a fungal disease called "damp-ing off," which occurs when seedlings are over-watered. To avoid it, allow your microgreens to dry off once per day before spraying them again. The whole tray shouldn't go bone-dry all the way through, but the microgreen leaves and stems should be free of water droplets for some time each day. In the absence of those water droplets, fungus has a difficult time growing and the greens can thrive.

Our Favorite Varieties

One of the fun parts of growing microgreens is experimenting with a ton of different vegetables and herbs to decide which you like best. Any plant with edible leaves can grow as microgreens, so get creative! Some of the most beautiful microgreens come from different colors of beets and Swiss chard. You also can grow onion microgreens to add an onion-y pop to dishes or try herby microgreens, such as cilantro and parsley. We mostly grow kale and collard microgreens for adding freshness to venison tacos. We also grow pea microgreens, which quickly produce big, crunchy shoots for salads.

Harvest and Preservation

To harvest your microgreens, wait until they reach your preferred size, then cut them at the base with a pair of sharp scissors. Imagine you're giving your microgreens tray a haircut. You can harvest most microgreens only once because you're trimming off the main growth point, but you can harvest certain microgreens, such as onions and peas, multiple times. They'll continue to grow back as long as you water them until they run out of stored energy. Microgreens are best when eaten fresh from the tray, but in a sealed plastic bag, they can keep in the refrigerator for around a week.

MICROGREENS SALAD

Depending on how many you grow, microgreens can function as a topping or the focal point of a meal. Big sturdy microgreens from radishes, sunflowers, and pea shoots make a great salad on their own. They also make excellent toppings for tacos or a substitute for sprouts in Southeast Asian dishes such as pad thai. This simple microgreens salad is a great side dish to accompany the rich flavors of steak or roasted mushrooms. The bright, lemony dressing and peppery radishes pair well with all kinds of microgreens, from kale to Swiss chard, so don't be afraid to experiment.

4 cups microgreens
½ cup radishes
½ cup toasted walnuts
1 lemon
3 tablespoons olive oil
Salt

1. Wash and drain the microgreens.

2. Slice the radishes.

3. To a medium mixing bowl, add the greens, radishes, and walnuts.

4. In a small mixing bowl, juice the lemon for 2 tablespoons of fresh juice.

5. Add the olive oil and salt to taste to the lemon juice. Stir to combine.

6. Pour the dressing over the salad and toss to coat evenly.

SALMON AVOCADO RICE BOWL WITH MICROGREENS

We love this dish in spring, when we're busy preparing the gardens for the growing season and need a quick, filling meal. The bright microgreens, fluffy rice, and fatty avocado and salmon make it a complete, hearty meal in a bowl. If you have a rice cooker, it only takes about 15 minutes of chopping and mixing to throw this together. To make it vegan, substitute mushrooms for the salmon.

⅔ cup uncooked white rice

1⅓ cups water

2 small salmon fillets

1 large carrot

1 avocado

1 tablespoon soy sauce

1 tablespoon vinegar

1 tablespoon honey

1 dash sesame oil

1 cup microgreens, such as spicy mustard, kale, and cilantro

1. Cook the rice according to package directions.

2. In a small pan over medium-high heat, sear the salmon until well-cooked, 4 to 6 minutes per side.

3. With a potato peeler or cheese grater, shave the carrot into thin strips.

4. Thinly slice the avocado.

5. In a small bowl, combine the soy sauce, vinegar, honey, and sesame oil.

6. Equally divide the rice, microgreens, avocado, carrots, salmon, and dressing between two bowls.

OYSTER MUSHROOMS

Per Pound
CALORIES: 184   **CARBS:** 31.2 g   **PROTEIN:** 13.1 g   **FAT:** 0.9 g
IMPORTANT MICRONUTRIENTS: vitamin D, ergothioneine

A few years ago, when we were living in a small third-floor apartment and trying to think of foods to grow indoors, we ordered a ready-to-fruit mushroom kit online to "produce your own bounty of oyster mushrooms on your kitchen table!" The kit cost $20, and after we added water and let it sit for a few weeks, it produced approximately 1 ounce of mushrooms— a hefty price tag for a measly harvest! These tabletop kits are fun for kids and allow new mushroom growers to get a feel for the process, but they don't work well for folks looking to save on grocery bills or sustain themselves by growing their own food.

After the tabletop kit, we considered excluding oyster mushrooms from our garden plans but decided to give them one more try. The next time, we ordered a bag of oyster mushroom "spawn"—meaning a grain colonized by oyster mushroom mycelium—and used it to create our own mushroom grow bags. We spread the bag of spawn, which cost the same as the tabletop kit, onto straw and ground-up cornstalks from our community garden, which produced pounds and pounds of oyster mushrooms over the next couple months. Since then, oyster mushrooms have become a vital part of our garden plan.

Oyster mushrooms (*Pleurotus spp.*) are some of the most widespread fungi on earth. They grow wild all over the globe, from the forests of North America to the mountains of East Asia, and they thrive on a wide variety of trees and plant materials. Many cultures have foraged and eaten them throughout history, but German soldiers reportedly first cultivated them intentionally during

World War I by growing them on the stumps of trees blown apart by artillery. Today you can find farm-grown oyster mushrooms in grocery stores and on restaurant menus around the world.

We primarily grow oyster mushrooms indoors through the winter, which provides us with a steady stream of fresh mushrooms in the colder months, when most of our food is canned, dehydrated, or frozen. In nature, oyster mushrooms grow on dead and dying hardwood trees. Their mycelium, similar to a plant's root system, releases enzymes that break down woody material, extract nutrition from it, and begin the process of converting it back to soil. They perform a similar duty in our gardens by breaking down old plant material like our cornstalks and straw. After the mycelium has digested the garden residue and finished producing mushrooms, we add the spent material to our compost pile, where the remaining mycelium, worms, and microbes break it down into a rich compost we can use in our garden beds in the spring.

Inoculation

To grow oyster mushrooms at home, you need a container, a growing medium, and spawn. We use cylindrical plastic grow bags purchased online, but any water-tight container will work if it's free of contamination. For the growing medium, oyster mushrooms have aggressive and adaptable mycelium that can grow on almost any dead plant material. In addition to cornstalks and straw, we've grown them successfully on rehydrated wood stove pellets, wild grasses, and hardwood logs. You *can* produce the spawn at home, using advanced techniques in a sterile environment. But if your house, like ours, is not sterile, we recommend that you purchase spawn online, which you can do for a very reasonable price. Our favorite retailer is Field & Forest Products, a small, family-owned company in Wisconsin from which we've been buying spawn for years.

Growing Conditions

Oyster mushrooms are a very aggressive fungus, which means they can outcompete many other wild fungi in the growing medium. Neverthe-

less, the first step is to pasteurize your growing medium. Heating your straw or cornstalks to 160°F for one hour destroys most of the fungal spores and bacteria naturally present on the medium. This step creates an environment primed for the oyster mushroom mycelium to thrive. Think of it like weeding a garden before you plant your crops: It knocks back the competition so your target crop can thrive.

To pasteurize our growing medium, we stuff the straw or ground cornstalks into an old pillow case and steam it in a large stockpot. After an hour of pasteurizing, lay your growing medium on a clean surface to allow it to cool until you can handle it safely. A plastic folding table works great for this step. If the growing medium is still hot and steaming when you add the spawn, you risk damaging or killing your oyster mushroom mycelium.

Another technique we use to prepare the growing medium is soaking it in a hydrated lime solution, which is just a mixture of ground limestone and water. The extremely high pH of this solution destroys most mold spores and bacteria, creating a perfect environment for oyster mushroom mycelium. To do this, we fill a container with the growing medium—again, the straw or chopped-up cornstalks—and cover it with the lime solution. We use ⅛ cup of hydrated lime per gallon of water. After it soaks for 18 to 24 hours, remove the growing medium from the solution and allow it to drain for about an hour.

After your growing medium has cooled from boiling or drained from lime soaking, sprinkle your spawn into it and mix it around. The amount of spawn you use is up to you, but for best results, the rule of thumb is to use 5 to 10 percent of the weight of your wet growing medium. If you have 20 pounds of wet straw, for example, use 1 to 2 pounds of oyster mushroom spawn.

After you mix your spawn into the growing medium, pack it into your containers. Press it in as densely as possible, packing it with your hands as you fill the container. When your container is full, seal it with a lid or, if you're using a bag, tie the end closed. Your bucket should have pre-drilled holes every 6 to 8 inches around the bucket to allow for oxygen exchange. For bags, cut small holes every 6 to 8 inches after tying off the end.

Now your containers are ready for the incubation period. The best conditions for incubation are a temperature in the high 70s and high humidity. To achieve this environment, we put our bags in large plastic bins next to our radiators. The radiator keeps the temperature high, while the lidded bin helps retain moisture and humidity. Once per day, we open the lid to let the spawn breathe and to check on progress. These are *ideal* conditions, so if you don't have a place in your home with the right temperature, it should still work, just more slowly. With the right conditions, though, the mycelium will take over the growing medium surprisingly quickly.

Keep the containers in the incubation area

Oyster mushrooms growing indoors

until white mycelium completely colonizes the growing medium, typically about three to five weeks. After a thick mass of white mycelium has tied the growing medium together sufficiently, move your containers to a fruiting chamber in the coolest area of your home. You can place them outside as long as outdoor temperatures are in the 50s or 60s F with high humidity. If you live in a low-humidity area, consider adding a humidifier to the setup. You can purchase one cheaply at most pharmacies or big-box stores.

Oyster mushrooms need some exposure to sunlight or grow lights to grow optimally. Without light, they'll grow stringy and pale. When growing them indoors, we use the same full-spectrum grow lights we use to start our seedlings in spring, which works excellently. If you don't have a grow light, place the fruiting mushrooms in a sunny window for good mushroom production.

Fungus gnats on a shiitake

Pests and Diseases

Fungus gnats sometimes affect oyster mushrooms grown indoors. These little critters look a lot like skinny fruit flies, and their tiny larvae chew through the mushrooms. They generally cause minimal damage that's hard to notice. If you're not vegetarian or vegan, a few fungus gnats provide a protein boost to the mushrooms.

Outdoors, you potentially face more pests, including slugs, snails, and fungus beetles, but for the most part, oyster mushrooms grow so quickly that you'll be harvesting them before the critters find them.

Our Favorite Varieties

We've had consistent success with Grey Dove and PoHu oyster mushrooms, both winter varieties that we typically grow in our basement through the cold months. Field & Forest Products sells other oyster mushrooms, some bred for growing in summer and others with beautiful yellow and pink flesh. Check those out and experiment with different varieties to determine what works best in your growing conditions.

Harvest and Preservation

You can dehydrate oyster mushrooms, but they lose a bit of their texture, so we preserve them by cooking them in oil or butter and freezing them in bags. Because we can grow them year-round, we typically don't do this unless we stumble on a big pile of them growing wild in the woods. Generally we only grow the amount we need at any one time and eat them as they grow.

POLENTA WITH OYSTER MUSHROOM RAGÙ

This meal is a go-to for us in the winter, when we're living off staple crops like grain corn polenta. The oyster mushrooms grow easily indoors, so we use them to keep some fresh produce in our diet when we're eating mostly preserved foods. Between the rich, filling polenta and the tangy oyster mushroom ragù, this meal checks all the boxes for a midwinter feast.

6 cups water, divided

1 pound oyster mushrooms

6 small garlic cloves

1 cup dry polenta or coarsely ground cornmeal

2 tablespoons butter

1 tablespoon vegetable oil

1 tablespoon fresh thyme

½ cup dry vermouth

½ cup fresh parsley

½ cup grated Parmesan cheese

Salt and pepper

1. In a medium pot over medium-high heat, bring 5 cups of water to a boil.

2. Meanwhile, tear or chop the oyster mushrooms into ½- to 1-inch pieces and mince the garlic. Set aside.

3. When the water is boiling, add the dry polenta while stirring vigorously to prevent clumping.

4. Reduce the heat to low, stir in the butter, and continue cooking until tender, about 40 minutes. Stir occasionally.

5. In a medium pan over medium-high heat, add the oil and mushrooms and sauté.

6. When the mushrooms begin to brown, stir them, add the minced garlic and thyme, and cook for 1 minute.

7. Add the vermouth and the remaining cup of water to deglaze the pan.

8. As the mushroom mixture thickens, stir it and sprinkle with parsley and Parmesan cheese.

9. Season both the polenta and ragù with salt and pepper to taste.

10. Allow the polenta to cool slightly so it begins congealing, then scoop some into a bowl and top with the ragù.

OYSTER MUSHROOM GRAVY

They don't contain much protein, but the texture and taste of oyster mushrooms makes them an excellent flavor replacement for meat. When Silvan was a vegetarian, she frequently found herself contemplating a menu, wondering if gambling on the one vegetarian entrée—usually some mushroom gravy or risotto dish—was worth it. So often they were disappointing: a mass of gray punctuated by blobs of bland button mushrooms. In the past decade, however, the world of mushrooms has expanded considerably, and many mushroom dishes no longer feel like a compromise. This flavorful gravy doesn't feel like settling at all, and we make it much more than any kind of meat gravy. Use whatever herbs suit your tastes or needs. Thyme and mushrooms make a wonderful pair. With potatoes, we might add rosemary or sage as well.

---

2 cloves garlic

1 medium red onion

4 tablespoons butter, divided

1 pound oyster mushrooms

½ cup dry red wine or sherry

2 cups vegetable broth, plus more if needed for consistency

1 tablespoon soy sauce

2 sprigs thyme or herbs of choice

2 tablespoons all-purpose flour

1 splash water

Salt and pepper

1. Mince the garlic and onion.

2. In a deep skillet over medium heat, melt 2 tablespoons of butter. Add the minced onion and cook until soft and just starting to brown, about 5 minutes.

3. Meanwhile, finely chop the oyster mushrooms.

4. Add the mushrooms, spreading them in a single layer, and cook without stirring until the undersides begin to brown, about 2 or 3 minutes.

5. Add the garlic and cook until it turns golden and fragrant, about 2 minutes.

6. Add the wine or sherry and stir vigorously to dislodge any brown bits stuck to the bottom of the pan.

7. Add the broth, soy sauce, and herbs and bring the mixture to a boil.

8. Reduce the heat to medium-low and simmer until the mixture reduces by about a third, about 10 minutes.

9. In a small bowl, whisk together the flour and a splash of water to make a slurry.

10. While continuing to stir the mixture, slowly add the slurry to the pan so it incorporates without lumps.

11. Increase the heat to medium-high and, stirring frequently, bring the mixture to a boil again.

12. When the gravy reaches your desired thickness, turn off the heat. Add the remaining 2 tablespoons of butter and salt and pepper to taste. If gravy is running too thick, whisk in more broth to achieve your desired consistency.

PEPPERS

Per Pound
CALORIES: 130.5   **CARBS:** 29.3 g   **PROTEIN:** 4.1 g   **FAT:** 1.7 g
IMPORTANT MICRONUTRIENTS: potassium, folate, vitamin A, carotenoids

If Silvan could grow only one plant in our garden, it would probably be peppers. Not only are they productive and easier to grow than their nightshade cousins, tomatoes and eggplant, but they also are beautiful plants worthy of any ornamental garden. They grow readily in containers and in small areas, making them versatile and valuable for home gardeners with limited space. We grow most of our peppers in nursery pots in our driveway, where they thrive with very little attention. People even grow small varieties indoors on sunny windowsills, something Jordan did in his freshman dorm room in college.

The pepper pots in our driveway

A habanero pepper

Sweet peppers

If you can take the heat, there's no better bang for your buck than growing hot peppers or chiles. Just a couple plants can produce enough fruit to spice up a year's worth of meals. Research indicates that, beyond that amazing warming sensation and mouth-watering flavor, the spicy sensation can be very good for you. Capsaicin, the compound responsible for chiles' famous burn, has potent anti-inflammatory and antioxidant effects. Scientists are even studying it for treating brain disorders and degenerative nerve diseases.

Humans have cultivated peppers for about 6,000 years, starting with gardeners in Central and South America. Spicy food with a high concentration of chiles is less susceptible to molding, so historians hypothesize that the spicy fruits initially helped preserve food in tropical climates, where mold can pose a big problem. Today we prize chiles less for their mold-

inhibiting properties and more for their flavor and heat. Chiles now grow in every corner of the world and make their way into Mexican salsa, Thai noodles, East African pili pili, and more.

Let's not forget sweet peppers, either; they also have an important place in our pantry. We grow a good number of assorted sweet peppers, including pimentos and Italian roasting peppers, which taste great fresh or canned or frozen for later. We add these peppers to pasta, stews, and salads, or grind them with walnuts and honey to make Muhammara (page 133), a delicious Syrian dip.

Seed Starting

Pepper seeds take a long time to germinate, so plan to sow them about two months before planting them outdoors after your average last frost date. Plant them about ¼ inch deep in moist potting soil. We usually plant two seeds per cell unless we're growing seeds that we know have a high germination rate. Peppers can be finicky about sprouting in cool temperatures, so ensure that they sprout reliably by keeping them in a warm area of your home, such as near a radiator or heat mat, until the seedlings push up from the soil. Even in ideal conditions, pepper seeds can take anywhere from one to three weeks to germinate.

After they emerge, transfer them immediately to a sunny window or under a grow light so they don't get leggy. We recommend moving them into a larger container at least once before planting them outside. We move ours from a small, 72-cell tray to 4-inch pots when they've grown their first set of true leaves. When they have a few sets of true leaves and are ready to go to their final home, transplant them into the ground or a 3- to 5-gallon container. Buckets with drainage holes drilled into the bottom can work well. Some compact pepper varieties can go into containers as small as 1 gallon for growing on patios or indoors.

Growing Conditions

Peppers like it humid and hot. Because we live in a relatively cool 6b growing zone, we grow our peppers in large black plastic pots in our driveway, and they thrive with the extra heat. They'll grow well anywhere they receive at least six hours of sun daily and plenty of warmth.

If you're growing your peppers in the ground, leave about 12 to 18 inches of space between each plant to give them adequate room to expand. We grow most of our peppers in containers, so we fill the containers two-thirds full of potting soil, with one-third compost, to keep them well-fed with nutrients throughout the growing season.

Tomato cages don't work well for most tomatoes because they don't contain the sprawling vines, but they are excellent for supporting pepper plants. Peppers aren't nearly as floppy as tomatoes, but they do tend to fall over under the weight of their fruit, so use some type of trellis to hold them upright and avoid broken stems. Tying the main stem to a simple wooden stake also does the trick.

Peppers are pretty hands-off until harvest. As long as they're receiving full sun, plenty of heat, and at least 1 inch of water per week, you should have no problems. If it hasn't rained recently, we water our containers thoroughly about twice a week. You can pick sweet and hot peppers green or allow them to mature to their ripe, colorful stage: red, yellow, or even purple. Green peppers are less flavorful than their colorful counterparts, but picking some green ones early can help encourage more fruit to form.

As the growing season wraps up and the first fall frost approaches, you'll likely still have some clusters of unripe peppers hanging from your plants. Peppers resist frost better than tomatoes and can survive light frosts with row covers, but when consistently freezing temperatures arrive, the plants will die. To make sure none of the fruit goes to waste, we cut the entire plants down at the base and hang the peppers in our basement, where they continue ripening for a few weeks. After they've all ripened or their skins are becoming soft and wrinkly, we harvest all the peppers to use or preserve.

Pests and Diseases

Peppers are generally pretty pest- and disease-free, but one common issue in pepper plants is blossom-end rot. This disease is exactly what

Trellised peppers

it sounds like: The blossom end of the pepper fruit turns brown and rots. The cause of this disease is a calcium deficiency in the plant, but that doesn't always mean that your soil lacks calcium. Inconsistent watering can result in calcium deficiencies. If your peppers consistently receive at least 1 inch of water per week and you still have blossom-end rot, consider adding a calcium-heavy fertilizer or supplement to improve the soil.

Our Favorite Varieties

When it comes to hot peppers, our favorite varieties are fish peppers, chile de árbol, Aleppo peppers, and jalapeños. The first three lend themselves well to dehydrating and grinding into chili flakes and chili powder. After jalapeños turn red, we like to smoke them before dehydrating them to make chipotle peppers, the perfect addition to any pot of beans or stew.

For sweet peppers, we always set aside space for Ashe County Pimentos. These extremely sweet, fleshy peppers are excellent roasted and do well when marinated and preserved. Italian heirloom frying peppers, such as Jimmy Nardello and Corno di Toro, are also staples for grilling and stuffing or for eating raw in salads.

Harvest and Preservation

One of the easiest ways of preserving chiles is hot sauce because half the flavor comes from vinegar. Most hot sauce recipes keep for a long time, espe-

cially when kept in a refrigerator. We love to use cayenne peppers and chili de árbol to make chili paste by blending them with salt, garlic, and olive oil. Without the preserving acid from the vinegar, this paste requires refrigeration, and you should use it all within a few months—but it tastes so delicious that we never have trouble with that!

Dehydrating chiles is our other go-to. We keep small ones whole and slice larger ones in half and throw them in the dehydrator at 125°F until crisp and completely dry, about 12 hours. Before

dehydrating them, putting them on a smoker for an hour or so will give them an amazing, smoky flavor. If you live in a particularly dry climate, you can simply string up your peppers by their stems and hang them to dry.

For sweet peppers, we typically chop, bag, and freeze them in serving-sized portions to defrost and use later for tacos, stews, and dips. We also roast, marinate, and can pimentos, which are delicious in an antipasto spread or pimento cheese.

MUHAMMARA

This is a sweet, savory, spicy dip from Aleppo, Syria. As with most of our recipes, we replaced many traditional ingredients with items we can grow or forage in Pennsylvania. (It's a lot easier to source honey here than to make pomegranate molasses, for example.) This dip makes an excellent appetizer with fresh pita or crackers.

3 large red bell peppers

1 cup shelled black or English walnuts

2 tablespoons olive oil, plus more for drizzling

1 tablespoon honey

1 clove garlic

1 teaspoon Aleppo pepper or chili powder

½ teaspoon salt

1. Cook the peppers under the broiler until the skin blisters and chars, turning to cook all sides evenly.

2. Place the charred peppers in a bowl and cover it with foil or a kitchen towel. Allow them to steam until the skin begins to peel from the flesh, about 10 minutes.

3. When the peppers have cooled enough to touch, remove the skin and roughly chop the peppers.

4. In a food processor, add all ingredients and pulse until the mixture combines well but still has some texture.

5. Top with a drizzle of olive oil and serve with toasted pita or crackers.

HOT SAUCE

When the mood suits us, we mix up this simple and basic recipe with different ingredients. Sweet peppers tone down the sharp heat from the chiles while still providing deep pepper flavor, for example. Try making it with a fruit or another sweet ingredient. We love adding peaches to ours. You can keep the ingredients raw before blending, but the texture will feel less smooth and the color will look less vibrant.

8 ounces medium hot peppers, such as cayenne or chile de árbol

4 ounces sweet peppers, such as paprika or pimento

1 or 2 teaspoons olive oil

1 cup apple cider vinegar

1 cup water

3 or 4 cloves garlic

1 teaspoon salt

1 teaspoon fresh ground black pepper

1. Stem, vein, and seed the peppers, if desired, for milder sauce. Roughly chop them.

2. In a large pan over medium heat, add the olive oil and chopped peppers and stir.

3. Add the remaining ingredients and simmer until the peppers become tender, about 10 minutes.

4. Remove from the heat, let cool for a few minutes, and transfer to a blender.

5. Blend until smooth and taste to adjust acidity or salt.

6. For extra smooth hot sauce, strain it through a fine mesh sieve. It will last several months in the refrigerator.

POTATOES

Per Pound
CALORIES: 419   CARBS: 97.2 g   PROTEIN: 8.8 g   FAT: 0.5 g
IMPORTANT MICRONUTRIENTS: potassium, sodium

To distinguish them from sweet potatoes, Americans sometimes call potatoes "Irish potatoes." This nod to the Great Famine tends to cause confusion about their origins. Potatoes were, in fact, first cultivated by farmers in the Andes Mountains, where they fueled the massive empire that built Machu Picchu and the Incan pyramids. There is a diverse array of varieties found in their home range where they are grown in terraced mountain gardens. Some estimates suggest that the Andes Mountains are home to around 4,000 unique varieties of potatoes. They range in color, shape, and size—from tiny, round, almost black tubers to elongated yellow ones that look more like bananas. Unfortunately, only a handful of these varieties made their way back to Europe before they became a widespread staple crop among working class people and tenant farmers in Ireland.

As students of history will remember, Ireland suffered a nationwide crop failure in the 1840s that tragically led to the deaths of nearly 1 million people and an exodus of one-quarter of Ireland's population. This crop failure was brought on by a fungal disease that heavily affected the primary variety of potatoes being grown, the Irish Lumper. During the Great Famine, wealthy British landowners in Ireland continued exporting peas, beans, honey, and other foods, and records indicate that Irish exports of butter, beef, and other commodities *increased* while tenant farmers and their families starved in the countryside among fields of rotting potatoes.

Putting the horrors of colonialism aside, potatoes make an excellent and reliable staple crop if grown using the traditional Incan practice of mixing many varieties together. If you rely on potatoes as your primary staple crop, growing an array of varieties ensures you'll harvest some, regardless of the growing conditions, due to genetic variability in disease resistance. Heirloom varieties like Adirondack Red and Magic Molly are resistant to late blight (*Phytophthora infestans*), so including them in your potato patch ensures that, even if this fungal disease strikes other varieties in your garden, you'll still harvest a bounty of red and blue potatoes that year.

In our gardens, potatoes form an important part of our staple crop repertoire. Jordan's dad, Rick, plants a rainbow of colorful varieties in our shared community garden plot, where they are more or less hands-off until harvest. Potatoes are easy to grow, store relatively well, and provide calorie-dense meals that stick to your ribs.

Seed Starting

Unlike many other crops in this book, potatoes are not propagated by seed but rather by cloning. The word "cloning" might conjure images of test tubes and other laboratory equipment, but cloning a potato is as simple as cutting off a chunk of the tuber and popping it in the ground.

> Because potatoes are propagated by cloning, the heirloom varieties in our gardens are not only the same species and variety as those grown by our gardening ancestors, but they are in fact the same individual plant we have collectively been keeping alive, through cloning, from year to year!

When preparing your potatoes for cloning, identify the "eyes" of the potato, which are the growth points from which the stalks, branches, and leaves grow. At first, these look like little dimples, but as they develop they begin to look like buds. Once you identify the eyes, cut up or "chit" your potatoes. Each chunk needs at least one eye to produce an entire plant. Avoid planting whole potatoes with many eyes because they'll crowd one another as they grow and result in stunted, anemic tubers.

Potatoes can grow directly in the ground or in raised beds or containers. Some people even grow them in piles of straw on bare soil, but we haven't attempted that method yet.

Growing Conditions

Potatoes need full sun and loose, well-draining soil to thrive. If your soil is heavy clay or densely compacted, you need to break it up and mix it with compost for the potatoes to develop properly. While potatoes need consistent watering, especially as their tubers develop, they can suffer from fungal disease if the soil becomes waterlogged. That's why a well-draining soil, a raised bed, or a large growing container is ideal for potatoes.

Many gardeners plant potatoes by digging a trench, placing the tubers in the bottom, and backfilling the soil as the plant grows. This technique works, but we find it to be unnecessary labor. In raised beds, we space our potatoes about 12 inches apart and plant them 6 inches deep. If any tubers push up and become exposed to sunlight later in the season, we backfill them with some surrounding soil or top them with mulch, but otherwise we just let them do their thing.

Depending on the variety, they can mature for harvest at different times of the year: early season, mid-season and late season. It's time to harvest mature potatoes when the aboveground plant growth dies back completely. Some new gardeners think they're losing their crop to a disease, but it's a normal part of their life cycle.

Pests and Diseases

The main insect pest you will contend with in your potato patch is the Colorado potato beetle (*Leptinotarsa decemlineata*). These beetles lay eggs on the leaves of potato plants, and their little red larvae gnaw through the foliage. They have poor camouflage, making them easy to remove by hand and susceptible to predators. Having a healthy population of predatory insects, such as wasps, in your garden is often enough to prevent a widespread outbreak.

As far as diseases to look out for in your potato beds, there is perhaps none more notorious than late blight, the cause of the Irish Potato Famine. The best tool for fighting it is well-draining soil and planting a diversity of potato varieties. While the tubers require regular mois-

Colorado potato beetle larvae

ture for optimal growth, soil that stays constantly wet or waterlogged is a prime environment for the fungal growth that leads to late blight. If you see brown and black lesions on the leaves, harvest your potatoes prematurely to avoid losing the whole crop.

Potato scab, another common fungal disease, also affects potato crops. It's mostly a cosmetic issue that causes marketing problems for commercial potato farmers. These potatoes won't win any beauty contests, but as long as you're OK with eating "imperfect" potatoes, don't worry too much about this disease.

Our Favorite Varieties

Our favorite varieties of potatoes are Kennebec, Red Pontiac, and Adirondack Blue.

Kennebec potatoes produce large white tubers with a delicious potato flavor, making them great for mashed potatoes or French fries. Red Pontiac

has red skin with white flesh that stores well, so we eat those later in the season. Adirondack Blue has dark blue skin and delicious blue flesh full of the same kinds of antioxidants as blueberries. All three are mid-season varieties, so we harvest them roughly at the same time. We enjoy these particular varieties, but it wouldn't be a bad idea to mix in a few early-season or late-season varieties when ordering your seed potatoes.

Harvest and Preservation

When your potato leaves begin to die back, but before they turn fully brown and dry, you can dig "new potatoes." These tubers haven't fully matured, so they have thin skins and a wonderful flavor and texture. Because their skins haven't formed fully, they don't store for very long, so eat them within a week or two of harvesting.

For storage-quality potatoes, wait until the aboveground plant growth has completely died back. At this point, the tubers have matured fully and formed a thick skin. When digging them up, always try to start your shovel or pitchfork at least 2 feet from the base of the plant to avoid cutting through any potatoes. No matter how hard you try, you *will* cut a few potatoes when digging them, but you can just wash those off and eat them that night.

If you plan to store your potatoes long-term, begin curing them right after harvest. Curing potatoes is simple, but keep a few critical points in mind. Don't wash your potatoes before curing because doing so likely will damage the skins, and the added water increases the chances of fungal issues in storage. You also don't want any light to reach your potatoes while they cure because it will turn them green, which renders them inedible. The best temperature for curing is between 45°F and 60°F with relatively high humidity. We cure them in our basement, which is the ideal place in our house.

After your potatoes have cured, you can leave them right where you cured them or load them into a paper bag, cardboard box, or sack and store them somewhere where no light will reach them until you're ready to eat them.

ROASTED POTATOES WITH FRESH HERBS

We tried many methods of roasting before landing on this one, which yields a crispy, golden exterior and soft, fluffy interior every time. Russet-style potatoes produce a crispier texture than more waxy varieties, such as Red Norland, but all taste delicious. Shower this side dish in whatever herbs you have in abundance— rosemary, parsley, basil, etc.—and serve it alongside venison steak or veggie burgers.

3 or 4 russet or Yukon gold potatoes

2 large cloves garlic

2 tablespoons high-heat oil, such as peanut or avocado

1 tablespoon salt

Freshly ground black pepper

1 large bunch parsley or herbs of choice

Grated Parmesan cheese (optional)

1. Wash and cut potatoes into 2- to 3-inch pieces.

2. In a large pot over medium-high heat, add the potatoes and cover them with water. Bring the water to a boil, reduce the heat to medium-low, and simmer them until they just start to feel tender, about 10 minutes.

3. Preheat the oven to 450°F and mince the garlic.

4. Drain the potatoes in a colander and rinse them with cool water to stop the cooking process.

5. Still in the colander, toss the potatoes to roughen their edges so they get nice and crispy in the oven.

6. In a medium mixing bowl, add the potatoes, garlic, oil, salt, and pepper to taste. Stir or toss to coat well.

7. On a baking sheet, spread the potatoes in an even layer and roast them until the outside edges turn brown and crispy, about 30 minutes.

8. Meanwhile, chop the parsley or herbs.

9. Remove the potatoes from the oven and top with the chopped parsley and, if desired, Parmesan cheese.

10. Serve hot with ketchup or, if you're feeling fancy, aioli.

KIMCHI LATKES

Fried potatoes take many delightful forms, but latkes remain one of our favorites. These fried potato pancakes became a staple among Jewish people in eastern Europe when potatoes reached the region in the 1700s, and they remain an important holiday staple to this day. They feel special, but they don't require much work. Adding some toppings can make them a complete meal on their own. Kimchi provides some nice spice and tang. If you decide to skip it, use a chopped onion in the mixture instead.

4 or 5 large russet potatoes

Salt

1 cup kimchi, plus more for serving

1 large egg

¼ cup breadcrumbs

Freshly ground black pepper

High-heat oil, such as peanut or avocado

Sour cream and chives for serving

1. With a box grater, shred the potatoes into a colander and sprinkle them with salt.

2. Chop the kimchi into ¼-inch-wide pieces and add it to the colander.

3. Place the colander in a larger bowl to save the starch that will drain with the liquid. Set a heavy bowl or other weight on the potatoes and kimchi to drain the excess moisture. Let drain for 10 minutes.

4. Meanwhile, preheat the oven to 200°F and, in a medium mixing bowl, lightly beat the egg.

5. Grab a handful of the potato-kimchi mixture, squeezing out any excess moisture, and transfer it to the mixing bowl.

6. After you've squeezed and transferred all the mixture, pour off the liquid from the bowl under the colander, saving the layer of pale, powdery starch at the bottom.

7. Add the potato starch to the mixing bowl and mix well.

8. Add the breadcrumbs and salt and pepper to taste and combine well. The batter should hold together but remain loose enough that individual strands of potato stick out.

9. In a cast-iron skillet or other heavy-bottomed pan, heat 1 or 2 inches of oil.

10. Make a small tester latke and lower it gently into the oil. If the oil is hot enough, it should sizzle immediately. Fry it until the underside turns golden brown, 1 to 2 minutes.

11. Flip it and fry on the other side until also golden brown, 1 to 2 minutes.

12. Taste your tester latke for seasoning and texture and adjust accordingly. If it's crumbly and falls apart too easily, add an additional egg to the batter. If it's too wet, add more bread-crumbs or 1 tablespoon of flour.

13. Form and fry the rest of the latkes, making sure not to over-crowd the pan.

14. Latkes taste best hot, so put the finished ones in the oven as you work your way through the batter.

15. Top with sour cream and chives and/or an additional spoonful of kimchi.

SHIITAKES

Per Pound Cooked
CALORIES: 374　**CARBS:** 64.8 g　**PROTEIN:** 7.0 g　**FAT:** 1.0 g
IMPORTANT MICRONUTRIENTS: vitamin D, potassium, ergothioneine

Like most crops in this book, the history of shiitakes started with people foraging them, eventually figuring out how to control their growth, then farming them. The difference with shiitakes is that they were first cultivated as recently as 800 years ago, compared with roughly 10,000 years ago for crops like corn and squash. Corn and squash look almost nothing like their wild counterparts, but the shiitakes at the grocery store look more or less identical to those that grow wild in the forests of East Asia. In their native range, shiitakes grow on trees in the oak family, called *shii* trees (*Castanopsis spp.*) in Japanese. For those of you who like etymology, *take* means "mushroom," so *shiitake* essentially translates to "oak mushroom."

After the initial work, growing edible mushrooms in your garden pays off for years. Think of shiitakes as a perennial crop, more like a peach tree than a potato plant. After you inoculate your logs, you can more or less just sit back and harvest a bounty of mushrooms whenever they fruit. Depending on the size of the logs, they can continue to produce mushrooms for four to eight years. Eventually the mycelium will completely break down the logs, leaving you with excellent brown compost.

Shiitakes form a critical part of our diet when we're living off the land. Mushrooms contain vitamin D, which is essential to a healthy diet when the sun hangs low in the winter sky. Many store-bought foods—including milk, cheese, and bread—are fortified with vitamin D, so we tend to take it for granted, but low vitamin D levels can lead to a weakened immune system, muscle pain, depression, and in extreme cases bone-related diseases, such as rickets. Our winter diet includes fish and organ meat from deer, both rich sources of vitamin D. If you're planning to live off the land without eating animal products, mushrooms are essential. Consider taking a vitamin D supplement in the winter as well.

Inoculation

Mushroom growing requires two elements: mycelium from the mushroom you want to grow and a medium on which to grow it. Mycelium, essentially the body of the mushroom, is sold commonly either as sawdust spawn or dowel spawn, which introduce the mycelium to the growing medium. Some mushrooms, such as oyster mushrooms, have very aggressive mycelium that can grow on pretty much anything. Shiitakes, however, prefer hardwood logs in the oak family, similar to the shii trees of East Asia.

Pittsburgh has a large number of mature oak and beech trees that arborists regularly trim to protect power lines. In winter and early spring, we keep a close eye on arborist trucks and snag any fresh-cut hardwood logs we can get our hands on. We want only fresh-cut logs from healthy trees because, as soon as a log is cut, the tree's immune system begins to fail, which creates openings for other wild fungi to colonize it. If you find a pile of logs that has been lying around for a few months, chances are high that another fungus has colonized the dead wood already and it will outcompete your shiitake mycelium. As a best practice, try to use logs within a month of being cut.

The best trees for shiitakes come from the oak family (Fagaceae) and include hardwood trees, such as oak, beech, and hornbeam. We've had success growing them on sugar maple, sweetgum, and mulberry logs, too. Avoid any evergreen trees like pine or spruce, though, as they contain antifungal compounds that prevent mushrooms from growing—this is what makes evergreen trees so good for untreated outdoor lumber.

Use a drill or modified angle grinder to cut holes into the logs every 4 to 6 inches. New mushroom growers should start with dowel spawn because all you need to insert that into the log is a handheld drill and hammer. Sawdust spawn requires a plunger to press the spawn into the holes. After you fill all the holes, seal them with beeswax or another food-grade wax to prevent them from drying out.

For the totem method, an entirely different style of inoculating logs, you need a chainsaw or large handsaw to cut the logs into sections

The mushroom logs in our yard

about 4 to 6 inches tall. Pile sawdust spawn onto each chunk, stack the next section upright, pile spawn on that, and so on. We've had success with this method for shiitake and lion's mane mushrooms.

Growing Conditions

After inoculating the logs, you need to wait at least six months before seeing any mushrooms. It seems like a long time, but think of it in terms of a perennial plant. You wouldn't expect to harvest a peach a month after you plant a peach tree, right? Like a perennial, your mushroom logs will produce for years as long as they stay moist and don't dry out completely. We keep our logs under a dense willow canopy in our side yard, which stays very moist, meaning that we hardly ever have to water them.

After 6 to 12 months, depending on the variety and the time of year you inoculated them, you can "force" your shiitakes into fruiting. Forcing means rapidly lowering their temperature so they think a cold spell has come, which shocks them into producing mushrooms. The most common way to do this is to submerge them in a tank of cool water for about 24 hours. After a couple

of days, you should begin to see tiny mushrooms "pinning" on the logs. Within a week, you'll be harvesting full-sized mushrooms. You can force your shiitakes around once a month, but give the logs time to recuperate in between. Otherwise, you can just allow your logs to fruit naturally, which will usually happen after a nice rainfall or during a shift in the weather.

Pests and Diseases

Shiitakes are generally pest-free. Little insects often use them for shelter, but most of the time you can simply brush them off and the mushrooms will be in perfect condition. Snails and slugs can cause some damage, though. Because of their slow nature and the ephemeral fruiting

Dehydrated shiitakes

of mushroom logs, they tend to catch on to the mushrooms only if they are left on the log too long. If you're having problems with slugs and snails, wait until a couple hours after dark, throw on a headlamp, fill a cup with salty water, and go on a slug hunt!

Our Favorite Varieties

Although shiitakes were only recently cultivated, there are a number of varieties with different traits to choose from. The three main types of shiitakes are cold weather, warm weather, and wide range. The names indicate when they prefer to fruit, with cold weather fruiting in winter, warm weather in early summer and early fall, and wide range throughout the year. Wide range shiitakes respond best to forcing, so we grow a lot of them, which helps us control when they produce mushrooms.

Harvest and Preservation

If you plan to eat your mushrooms right away, brush off any insects and dirt with a dry brush, cut them up, and cook them. Don't wash or rinse mushrooms because they soak up water like a sponge, which can make them a bit less palatable when cooked. If you have a surplus of mushrooms and want to store some, dehydrate them and store them in airtight jars. When you are ready to use them, rehydrate them by pouring some hot water over them, and they're ready to use just like fresh mushrooms. Save the rehydrating water, too, as it makes a great mushroom broth.

Regardless of how you use your mushrooms, though, we recommend sitting them in the sun for a couple hours before eating or storing them. Just like us, they synthesize vitamin D when exposed to sunlight. Even just a few minutes of sunlight exposure can increase their vitamin D content significantly.

SHIITAKE WALNUT BURGERS

Until we started hunting, Silvan was a vegetarian for most of her life and still appreciates a good veggie burger. Don't think of them as substitutes for something else, though. Look at them as a great, creative way to pack a lot of vegetables into one dish and celebrate interesting flavors. These walnut-mushroom burgers combine a bounty of fall and winter ingredients. The walnuts give them a satisfying crunch and richness, and the shiitakes impart a meaty, umami flavor. For a classic burger experience, serve these with Roasted Potatoes with Fresh Herbs (page 143) and a Microgreens Salad (page 113), with some pickles and homemade ketchup and mustard on the side. Make a large batch ahead of time and freeze them to reheat later.

---

2 cups shiitakes

1 clove garlic

1 egg

3 Tbsp olive oil, divided

1 tablespoon honey

1 splash soy sauce

½ cup walnuts of choice

1 tablespoon miso paste

½ cup Roasted Winter Squash (page 168)

1 teaspoon chili powder

Salt and pepper

1 cup all-purpose flour, plus more (optional) for coating

Breadcrumbs (optional)

1. If using dried mushrooms, cover them with boiling water, let them soak for 15 minutes, and drain. If using fresh, skip this step.

2. Mince the garlic. In a small bowl, lightly beat the egg. Set aside.

3. Dice the mushrooms into ¼-inch pieces.

4. In a skillet over medium-high heat, sauté the mushrooms in 1 tablespoon of the oil until golden brown, about 10 minutes.

5. Add the garlic and cook until it softens and becomes fragrant, 5 minutes.

6. Add the honey and soy sauce, stir to combine, and transfer the mushroom mixture to a medium mixing bowl to cool.

7. Using a molcajete or mortar and pestle, pound the walnuts. You can use a food processor, but the molcajete produces a better texture and is more fun! Combine with the miso paste.

8. Add the walnut-miso mixture, winter squash, chili powder, and salt and pepper to taste to the mushrooms and stir to combine well.

9. Stir in the egg and flour and chill for 20 to 30 minutes.

10. Meanwhile, preheat the oven to 200°F.

11. In a skillet over medium heat, add 2 tablespoons of oil.

12. Form the chilled mixture into patties.

13. If desired, dredge the patties in more flour or breadcrumbs for a crispier exterior.

14. Cook each patty until the outside browns, 2 or 3 minutes per side. Keep them warm in the oven until ready to serve.

SHIITAKE TOAST

This recipe works with any mushrooms, but the meaty texture and earthy flavor of shiitakes make them a perfect pairing for tangy, sharp cheddar cheese and hearty bread. We like to throw this dish together for an easy party snack or just as a meal on its own when we harvest a big pile of shiitakes and don't know what to do with all of them!

4 cups shiitakes

1 tablespoon water

2 tablespoons olive oil, plus more for brushing

1 tablespoon balsamic vinegar

1 tablespoon soy sauce

6 slices crusty bread, such as sourdough

6 slices sharp cheddar cheese

Flaky sea salt to taste

1. Preheat the oven to 350°F and cut the shiitakes into ¼ -inch slices.

2. In a medium lidded pan over medium heat, add the mushrooms and water. Cover and cook until the mushrooms shrink a little and start to cook through, 3 to 5 minutes.

3. Uncover, add the olive oil, and stir.

4. Increase the heat to medium-high and cook, stirring occasionally, until the mushrooms begin to brown, 5 to 10 minutes.

5. Add the balsamic vinegar and soy sauce and stir to coat evenly.

6. With more oil, brush the 6 spots on a baking sheet where you'll place the bread to toast.

7. On the prepared baking sheet, lay the bread slices and pile a few scoops of mushrooms on each slice.

8. Top each pile of mushrooms with a slice of cheddar cheese.

9. Bake until the cheese thoroughly melts and the bread toasts. Sprinkle with salt to taste and serve.

SPINACH

Per Pound
CALORIES: 126 **CARBS:** 11.9 g **PROTEIN:** 13.1 g **FAT:** 2.7 g
IMPORTANT MICRONUTRIENTS: iron, magnesium, potassium, vitamin C, vitamin A, folate

During the Great Depression in the United States, many children suffered from malnourishment because they lacked access to micronutrient-dense foods. Most families were subsisting exclusively on foods like cornmeal, potatoes, and beans, which are full of important macronutrients like protein, carbohydrates, and fats, but fresh fruits and green vegetables were expensive and harder to come by. One solution to this problem was a micronutrient-dense green vegetable that was cheap to produce and could be stored and shipped long distances: canned spinach. This micronutrient powerhouse provided a remedy to the childhood nutrient deficiency, but as you might imagine, few children were excited about the new pile of green mush on their plates. Enter Popeye the Sailor Man.

E. C. Segar, creator of the Popeye series, wanted to encourage malnourished kids to eat micronutrient-dense spinach, and what better way than to make their favorite superhero ravenous for it? The superhuman effect that canned spinach had on Popeye contributed to an explosion in canned spinach sales, with some estimates suggesting that, during the 1930s, spinach consumption increased by 33 percent. This marketing campaign had serious sticking power, too. Even in the 1990s, we both grew up eating spinach to make us "strong like Popeye."

Jordan also grew up eating spinach in Syrian fatayer, or spinach pies, which long predate the era of Popeye and go all the way back to the origins of the crop. Spinach was likely first cultivated in what is now Iran, Iraq, and Syria, where it was eaten for thousands of years before it took the world by storm through global trade. Nowadays, spinach fills saag paneer in India

and accompanies artichokes in cheese dip in the United States. At this point, it's hard to imagine spinach as an uncommon, regional food.

But the ubiquity of spinach is well-deserved. As Popeye would correctly tell you, its leaves are rich in iron, potassium, fiber, and antioxidants. It is also a very cold-hardy green, and it often survives our frigid western Pennsylvania winters, which allows us to have fresh green salads in winter, when most other crops in the garden are dormant.

Seed Starting

Getting the seeds to sprout can be one of the most challenging parts of growing spinach. It is notoriously picky about when it will emerge from its seed. Additionally, if you sow it directly into your garden beds, the chunky seeds make an attractive little snack for insects and birds, which will sometimes pick through the soil until they eat it all.

To ensure good germination, start the seeds inside in plug trays with moist potting soil. When they have two or three true leaves, transplant them into the garden. If you're having trouble getting the seeds to germinate in the potting soil, try folding some seeds in a damp paper towel and placing them in a warm spot inside your home. As long as you keep the paper towel damp, the seeds will sprout in a couple days, and you can transfer them to the plug trays. When you do, plant them about ½ inch deep in the moist potting soil.

Growing Conditions

Spinach is a cool weather crop, and most varieties struggle in hot weather. If you live in a cool, mild climate, spinach will do well in most seasons. For regions with hot summers and freezing winters, plant spinach in early spring and fall.

Under row cover, spinach survives in our garden all winter, but as soon as the warm days and nights of summer come, the spinach shoots up a flower stalk and tries to produce seeds, which is called "bolting."

Two factors trigger spinach bolting: day length and temperature. Some varieties, marketed as bolt-resistant or heat-tolerant, will outlast other types of spinach in summer, but eventually they, too, will succumb to the warm weather and long days. They say that you should "make hay while the sun shines," but in the case of spinach, make it while it *doesn't*.

Pests and Diseases

The most common insect pests for spinach are leafminers and spinach flea beetles. Leafminers (*Pegomya spp.*) lay their eggs on the leaves, and when they hatch, the larvae tunnel through the leaves, causing extensive damage. Because the leaf miner larvae are protected inside the leaves, pesticides are typically ineffective against them. To control their population, examine damaged leaves until you find the larvae, then squish them inside the leaves, trying not to damage the plant too much in the process.

Spinach flea beetles (*Disonycha xanthomelas*) leave small white dots on the spinach leaves, but their damage is mostly cosmetic. You can reduce flea beetle populations by covering your spinach beds in row cover, which provides a physical barrier that prevents the flea beetles from accessing your spinach in the first place. As long as you're not trying to sell your spinach at a farmers' market, don't worry too much about this cosmetic damage.

Our Favorite Varieties

Two of our go-to Spinach varieties are Bloomsdale Longstanding and Sunangel F1. Bloomsdale Longstanding is a hardy spinach whose thick leaves can withstand freezing winters and pro-vide excellent late fall or winter harvests. Sunangel F1 is a hybrid variety that is bred for bolt resistance in the sunny summer months. Like any spinach, it will eventually bolt, but it will outlast many other varieties in warm weather.

Harvest and Preservation

For full-sized leaves, spinach takes about 40 to 50 days from seeding to reach maturity, but you can pick the leaves as baby spinach whenever you like. Spinach is a cut-and-come-again crop, so as long as you harvest leaves from the outside of the rosette, the plant will keep pushing out new leaves until it bolts. If kept free of excessive moisture, spinach leaves can stay fresh in the refrigerator for up to two weeks.

For long-term storage, we blanch our spinach, squeeze it into baseball-sized portions, and freeze those in gallon bags. Blanching destroys enzymes that will discolor the leaves and degrade the flavor and texture, even in the freezer. Whenever we want some spinach in winter, we just pull out a ball, defrost it, and throw it in a pan.

SYRIAN SPINACH PIES
[FATAYER]

Jordan's family eats these delicious spinach pies as a staple, and they're one of our favorite ways to use up a big spinach harvest. Tangy spinach filling inside crispy, buttery dough makes them perfect for almost every occasion, from summer cookouts to winter feasts. They also freeze well, so when we have a lot of spinach available, we make huge batches, freeze them, and defrost them through the year as needed. If you like it spicy, top them with chili flakes.

FOR THE DOUGH

3 cups all-purpose flour

1 tablespoon active dry yeast

1 teaspoon salt

1 cup warm water

⅓ cup olive oil

FOR THE FILLING

4 large bunches spinach leaves, or about 2 lbs.

1 medium yellow onion

1 teaspoon olive oil, plus more for greasing

1 lemon

1 teaspoon salt

1 tablespoon ground allspice

1. In a medium mixing bowl, combine all the dough ingredients to form a sticky ball.

2. Cover the bowl, put it in a warm place, and let the dough rise until it doubles in size, about 1 hour.

3. Meanwhile, make the filling. Roughly chop the spinach and finely chop the onion.

4. In your largest pan over medium heat, add the olive oil and onions and cook until translucent, about 5 minutes.

5. Juice the lemon for 2 tablespoons of fresh juice. Set aside.

6. Working in batches if needed, add the spinach to the pan to wilt.

7. When all the spinach has wilted fully, add the salt, allspice, and lemon juice. Stir to combine and turn off the heat.

8. Preheat the oven to 375°F and, on a floured surface, roll out the dough to ¼ inch thick.

9. With a cookie cutter or drinking glass, cut the dough into circles.

10. Stretch the dough circles until you can almost see through them.

11. Add 1 tablespoon of the spinach filling to each dough circle and fold the sides to form a triangle.

12. Grease a baking sheet with olive oil, add the fatayer, and bake until they turn golden brown, about 15 minutes.

SPINACH EGGS
[PAN LUNCH]

This is a meal that was born out of convenience/desperation when Jordan was working as an apprentice on a research farm in rural North Carolina. The farm was a 20-minute drive from the nearest grocery store, and the apprentices didn't have regular access to a vehicle to get there, so store-bought food was sometimes scarce. They did have plenty of eggs from the farm chickens and greens from the garden, however. On their lunch break, they quickly and easily threw together this dish, which Jordan dubbed "pan lunch." With feta cheese and some toasted bread, it makes a wonderful, satisfying meal.

1 tablespoon olive oil, divided
5 cups spinach leaves
4 eggs
½ cup crumbled feta cheese
½ tablespoon hot chili flakes
Salt and pepper
4 slices toast (optional)

1. In a medium lidded pan over medium-high heat, add ½ tablespoon of olive oil and wilt the spinach until you can stir it around with a spoon.

2. Spread the spinach in an even layer and, with a spoon, make 4 divots in it. Divide the remaining ½ tablespoon of olive oil equally among the divots.

3. Crack an egg into each divot.

4. Over the eggs and spinach, sprinkle the feta cheese, chili flakes, and salt and pepper to taste.

5. Cover and cook until the eggs cook to your liking, 4 to 5 minutes.

6. If desired, scoop some spinach and an egg onto a piece of toast.

SQUASH

Per pound of winter squash:
CALORIES: 225 **CARBS:** 48.6 g **PROTEIN:** 11.2 g **FAT:** 2.8 g
IMPORTANT MICRONUTRIENTS: beta-carotene, vitamin A

Per pound of summer squash:
CALORIES: 90 **CARBS:** 19.4 g **PROTEIN:** 4.1 g **FAT:** 1.4 g
IMPORTANT MICRONUTRIENTS: vitamin A

Few crops capture the spirit of fall abundance quite like a big pile of squash. They are prominently featured in cornucopia paintings celebrating autumnal bounty and piled high as fall decorations every October in a nod to the harvest seasons of yesteryear. The English word *squash* comes from the Narragansett *askutasquash,* which roughly translates to "that which is eaten raw"—an interesting tidbit of etymology because people so rarely eat them raw now.

Around 10,000 years ago, in what is now Mexico, people first cultivated squash, and it has been an important staple crop for people in North America ever since. In the past few hundred years, global trade has introduced squash to cuisines around the world. Jordan grew up eating koosa, an heirloom summer squash bred in Syria, Palestine, and Lebanon hundreds of years ago. Koosa now forms an integral part of Arab food culture, but like all squash, its origins began in the Americas. Over the past hundred years, the Arab diaspora brought koosa back to its birthplace in Mexico, where it now goes by the name *calabacitas.* Quite the world traveler!

Squash prolifically produces large bulky fruits that are rich in carbohydrates, micronutrients, and dietary fiber. Its wide leaves and sprawling vines provide excellent water retention and weed suppression for the entire garden. Winter squash, one of our most important staple crops, allows us to produce hundreds of pounds of food in some of the least accessible parts of our gardens. In Pittsburgh, our yards and community gardens are typically built on sharply sloping hills, which means large chunks of potential growing space can be difficult to cultivate and manage. Our solution to make use of these steep hills in our gardens is to plant vining winter squash along the top and allow them to meander down the hills to produce fruit over the summer. We plant several on the steep hill in our front yard, and it's always a big hit with the neighbors, especially when the tan pumpkins start forming and changing color. Kids love that we have our very own pumpkin patch, which is a great way to strike up a conversation about gardening with your neighbors! In late fall, with boots on, we carefully navigate the tangled, vine-covered hillside to harvest hundreds of pounds of mature winter squash to cure and store for winter.

Squash is an incredibly dynamic crop, and it comes in lots of unique shapes, sizes, and

colors, from tiny yellow summer squash to monstrous competition pumpkins. The largest recorded pumpkin weighed 2,700 pounds, about the same size as a Honda Civic. In our gardens, we primarily grow an old heirloom variety we call Carolina Princess. The seeds came from Silvan's mom's garden in North Carolina, and we've been saving seeds and selecting for favorable traits in our garden for years. At this point, the pumpkins have adapted perfectly to our northern environment and produce piles of storable food each year.

We slice and roast squash for a side dish, cube it for venison stew, purée it to make pumpkin bread, and even put half a cup of cooked pumpkin in our dog's food every night, which she loves. If growing conditions are optimal, squash can be one of the most hands-off, productive crops in the garden.

Seed Starting

You can start squash, like corn and beans, either directly in the garden or in trays for transplanting. Trays are only necessary if you need to start them indoors to extend your season. Many vari-

eties of winter squash take more than 100 days to reach full maturity, so if you live in a far northern climate, start them indoors and transplant them after your average last frost date.

If you have a long growing season, simply pop a squash seed in the ground, keep it watered, and you'll have a sprawling bush or vine in no time. We throw a shovelful of compost on each spot where we want to grow a squash vine, then plant two or three seeds 1 inch deep in the compost. In warm conditions, your squash plant will burst through the soil in as little as a few days, but in cooler conditions it can take up to 10 days to germinate. If you use the compost technique, make sure the compost stays moist through irrigation or rainwater until the plant has established its roots in the soil beneath the compost, which usually takes about two weeks.

Growing Conditions

When deciding where to locate your squash plants, remember that squash needs full sun, at least six hours per day, to grow optimally. Good sunlight exposure also helps prevent fungal diseases from affecting the leaves later in the season.

Squash has large, wide leaves that tend to lose a lot of moisture during the hot parts of the day. When the sun is high, this temporary wilting can make it look like the squash plants are dying, but they'll perk back up when it cools off in the evening. This cycle can alarm new gardeners, but as long as the squash is recovering in the cooler parts of the day, it is most likely receiving adequate water. In general, you should try to ensure that it receives at least 1 inch of rainwater or irrigation per week.

The wide, sprawling leaves also allow for excellent water retention in the soil, squash's main contribution to a Three Sisters plot. As we discussed in the Companion Planting chapter (page 29), we plant a few squash vines at the base of our corn and beans. After they establish themselves, the squash leaves do such a good job preventing rainwater evaporation from the soil in our region that we usually don't need to water the Three Sisters plots at all for the rest of the season.

You can also plant squash on its own in rows or patches. A designated squash or pumpkin patch will produce a lot more fruit than the Three Sisters vines because the plants aren't competing for sunlight with tall cornstalks and vining beans. To ensure a good crop of winter squash, we usually dedicate a small patch of the garden to exclusively grow squash vines. As we mentioned earlier, the steep hills of our gardens are perfect for this purpose since they would otherwise be left fallow.

Pumpkin vines in our front yard

Pumpkin leaves wilting during the day

We grow primarily winter squash or pumpkin, but we believe that summer squash also deserves some space in the garden. The growing conditions for summer squash are fairly similar, with the primary difference being that winter squash typically sprawls as a vine and summer squash stays put as a bush. So space winter squash plants a little farther apart than summer squash. Space your winter squash at 2 to 3 feet between plants, and summer squash 1½ to 2 feet between plants. When your winter squash vines take over the area—and they will—train them to grow where you want by dragging the end of the vine in the direction you want it to grow.

Squash and pumpkins have male and female reproductive organs on separate flowers, which means that insects need to pollinate them to produce fruit. If, for whatever reason, your garden lacks insects, unpollinated fruit embryos might rot and fall off the plant before maturing. In this case, you will want to hand-pollinate the flowers. Collect some pollen grains from a male flower with a dry paintbrush and spread them inside a female flower. For a more long-term solution, dedicate some space in your garden plan to native plants that attract pollinators.

Pests and Diseases

The two primary pests that you will battle in your squash patch are the aptly named squash bug and squash vine borer. Squash bugs (*Anasa tristis*) are sap-sucking insects that lay their eggs on squash leaves so their larvae can feed on the plants as they develop. Both the adults and larvae suck sap from the leaves and stems, which can be detrimental to fruit production and even kill the plant in large enough numbers. These bugs overwinter in squash debris, so you can control them from year to year by removing and composting dead squash plants at the end of the season. Check your plants periodically and scrape any unhatched eggs off the leaves with your fingernail or pull them off with a piece of tape.

Squash vine borers (*Melittia cucurbitae*) are orange and black moths who lay their eggs at the base of squash plants so their maggot-like larvae can tunnel and eat the vine from the inside out. Their boring results in what looks like sawdust spilling out of your squash vines. If you find it

Insects in a pumpkin flower

early enough, you can perform a little bit of field surgery to remove the grubs by slicing the hollow vines open vertically and pulling out the larvae with tweezers. If you use this method, make sure to cover the incision with soil or garden tape afterward to allow the vine to heal.

To keep both these insects off your plants, cover them with row cover or insect netting when the plants are still young. Squash needs insects to pollinate it, though, so remove the cover as soon as your plants start flowering to allow pollinators in.

The most common diseases to impact squash plants are powdery mildew and blossom-end rot. Powdery mildew appears as a blotchy white substance that coats the leaves and eventually causes the plant to wilt and die. New growers sometimes confuse the natural white marks on zucchini and other squash varieties with powdery mildew, but powdery mildew sits on the leaves and can be wiped away, whereas the natural white splotches can't. After you observe the differences a few times, they become easy to differentiate. If you live in an area with high humidity and frequent rainfall, you likely will experience powdery mildew at some point in the season, hopefully *after* harvesting a big pile of squash! Many varieties of squash are resistant to this disease, which can buy you time before your plant succumbs to the blight. When selecting your seeds, look for varieties that say "powdery mildew resistant" or "PM resistant."

Blossom-end rot is exactly what it sounds like. The blossom end of your squash will develop a black spot that eventually spreads and rots the whole fruit. A calcium deficiency or lack of water often causes this disease, so if you see it, make sure you're watering consistently and, for a long-term solution, consider amending your soil with a calcium-rich fertilizer, such as bone meal.

Squash vine borer larvae and their damage, and an adult moth

Our Favorite Varieties

As I mentioned earlier, our favorite squash is the Carolina Princess pumpkin that we save seeds from every year. This section is meant to provide you with suggestions for which seeds to grow, and we have no idea where you could get these unless you run into us somewhere and we happen to have some on us. Instead, we'll advise you to seek out fellow gardeners growing heirloom varieties and ask to trade for some seeds. Because squash seeds are so easy to save, with enough space you can have your own heirloom variety in a few years! See the Seed Saving chapter (page 51) for more information.

For butternut squash, a classic that many people know and love, Waltham is a great variety to grow if you're new to winter squash and want something productive, sweet, and highly storable. Jordan's family loves koosa—a Syrian, Palestinian, and Lebanese heirloom summer

Powdery mildew beginning and spreading

Normal white pattern on squash leaf

variety—which they core and stuff with meat and rice. The seeds are available in a growing number of seed catalogs, and we recommend giving it a try if you like summer squash but want something a little different from the typical American version.

Finally, yellow crookneck and zucchini are the two most commonly grown squash varieties by gardeners in the United States. They are excellent for beginners because they produce prolifically, provide you a consistent summer harvest, and taste delicious on the grill.

Harvest and Preservation

First, a note of caution: Squash vines have a protective fuzz that irritates the skin and causes itching for a couple hours after harvesting, so wear pants and long sleeves, or take care not to let the leaves and stems rub your bare skin.

When it comes time to harvest, the fruit comes on fast. Summer squash ripens first. Once it does, you'll be harvesting from the plants every other day. We pick summer squash at about 6 to 8 inches long, the point at which the majority of varieties taste the most tender. If you find a giant, overgrown fruit on your summer squash it won't be much good on the grill, but it will make great zucchini bread.

As the air cools and summer winds down, your winter squash and pumpkins will begin to mature. They can reach their full size weeks

Zucchini forming

before maturing, but in an immature state, they don't store as long or taste as good. To ensure your winter squash and pumpkins have reached maturity, feel the stem. Think of the stem as the fruit's umbilical cord. It sends nutrients to the fruit, and as it does, the stem remains soft, flexible, and light green. After the plant finishes transporting nutrients to the fruit, the stem dries down and becomes hard and woody. That's when we like to harvest our winter squash. Cut the stem about 2 to 3 inches above the top of the fruit to ensure it seals completely.

We cure ours on a shelf in our basement to store for winter. Curing just entails allowing your winter squash to sit in a warm, well-ventilated area for a few weeks until their skin darkens a bit and the stem becomes fully dry and woody. In that cured state, winter squash can store at room temperature for up to a year.

ROASTED WINTER SQUASH

Caramelized roasted squash, a simple staple in our home, makes a perfect side dish for venison steak, A Really Good Pot of Beans (page 66), or mixed into a bowl of mac and cheese. For each winter squash, we roast half for ourselves and bake the other half for our dog's food. (Because the recipe below contains garlic, it's just for humans, not dogs.)

1 medium winter squash or pumpkin

4 cloves garlic

2 tablespoons olive oil

1 tablespoon ground coriander

1 tablespoon smoked paprika

1 teaspoon salt

1. Preheat the oven to 375°F.

2. Slice the squash into ½-inch disks and mince the garlic.

3. In a large mixing bowl, combine all ingredients and stir to coat evenly.

4. On a large baking sheet, spread the squash slices in an even layer and roast them until they caramelize, about 30 minutes.

PUMPKIN SEED SALSA MACHA

This delicious, easy dish from the Veracruz region of Mexico has it all: crunch, flavor, heat, and tang. It's extremely versatile, so after you've made our version, have fun experimenting with different ingredients from your garden or region.

½ cup olive or other vegetable oil, plus 1 tablespoon

15 to 20 small dried hot chiles, such as chile de árbol

½ cup raw pumpkin seeds

2 or 3 large cloves garlic

1 teaspoon cumin seeds or powder

1 teaspoon salt

2 tablespoons apple cider vinegar

¼ cup roasted pumpkin (optional)

1. In a medium pan over medium heat, add the oil and chiles and toast them, stirring frequently so they don't burn. When they have browned in places and become fragrant, about 5 minutes, transfer them to a food processor or high-powered blender.

2. Add 1 more tablespoon of oil to the pan, followed by the pumpkin seeds, and cook until the pumpkin seeds brown lightly, 2 to 3 minutes.

3. Meanwhile, mince the garlic.

4. Add the garlic and cumin to the pan and cook, stirring frequently, until the garlic becomes golden and crunchy, about 2 minutes.

5. Transfer the garlic and seed mixture to the food processor and add the salt, vinegar, and, if desired for creamy sweetness, the roasted pumpkin.

6. Pulse to incorporate and roughly chop all ingredients into small pieces, but don't overpulse to a purée. You want to preserve that crunchy texture.

7. Adjust salt and vinegar to taste and store in an airtight container in the fridge for up to a month.

SWEET POTATOES

Per Pound
CALORIES: 342   CARBS: 79.6 g   PROTEIN: 6.2 g   FAT: 0.6 g
IMPORTANT MICRONUTRIENTS: magnesium, potassium, vitamin C, vitamin A, vitamin K, beta-carotene

Silvan grew up in North Carolina, the number one state for sweet potato production, a fact she likes to bring up whenever the plant is mentioned. As such, sweet potatoes hold a special place in our hearts. Years ago, when we ran our own small farm there, we grew a lot of them. It was always hard not to dig them too early, staying patient until the first frost of the year, when we would finally get to see whether our harvest would be bountiful. Now that we live farther north, we grow more winter squash than sweet potatoes, but we still save some room for these beautiful and nutritious plants. Sweet potato leaves are also edible and make a great summer green when it's too hot for spinach. We enjoy the leaves and the roots in curries and stews, where the roots' firmer texture holds up much better than pumpkin flesh.

Despite their name in English, sweet potatoes are related to other potatoes only very distantly. They also aren't a tuber but a true root, meaning that, if left to grow with enough water and nutrients, they keep getting bigger. The largest one on record weighed in at more than 81 pounds!

The wild cousin of sweet potatoes is a perennial vine native to Central and South America, but now it's mostly grown in its cultivated form as an annual vegetable. Historians believe that farmers first cultivated them as an annual food crop at least 5,000 years ago, and they have served as important evidence in piecing together the history of intercontinental exploration. Through DNA analysis, researchers have proven that the humble sweet potato made its way from the Andes Mountains in South America all the way to Polynesia almost 1,000 years ago. Since then, sweet potatoes have made their way into numerous cuisines across the globe and are hugely popular in Asia and West Africa. The United Nations Food and Agriculture Organization actively encourages production of sweet potatoes in areas with high rates of malnutrition because its high yields and high levels of beta-carotene and other vitamins make it an extremely efficient staple crop.

Seed Starting

Rather than growing from seeds, sweet potatoes are traditionally grown from "slips," a sprout grown from the mature root. In spring, you can buy slips from many local garden centers or farm supply stores, or you can order from a larger selection of varieties online. (Tater Man in Georgia has a great name and a large selection.) It's also simple to make your own slips from store-bought sweet potatoes or

garden-grown ones from the previous year. If using store-bought, choose organic sweet potatoes because these are less likely to have been sprayed with a growth inhibitor that prevents sprouting. We've grown slips in two ways: the water method and the soil method.

The water method doesn't require much in the way of materials, but it does take longer, sometimes up to two months. You need a jar, toothpicks or paper clips, and a sunny windowsill. Fill a jar halfway with water. Stick toothpicks or straightened paper clips into the non-rooting end of a sweet potato so that it hangs in the jar with a few inches underwater and a few above water. The rooting side tapers to a point and may have small, dry root pieces hanging from it. Submerge the sweet potato, rooting side down. Put your jar in a warm, sunny spot and add more water as needed. Change the water weekly so it doesn't get too funky. From the sides or top of the potato, sprouts should emerge in a few weeks. Let them grow to 4 or 5 inches long with a few leaves, then gently twist them off the sweet potato. If they already have roots, plant them right away. If not, put them in a fresh jar of water in the same spot and wait for roots to develop before planting.

The soil method results in faster slip development, usually three to four weeks, but it requires more space and usually supplemental lighting. If you're already set up for spring seed starting, you have everything you need! In an open seedling tray or other shallow container with drainage holes, spread a layer of potting soil. Lay your sweet potatoes horizontally in the tray and fill with more potting soil to cover them about two-thirds of the way up. Place the tray in a warm spot with bright light either from a window or grow lights. A heated soil mat will accelerate the process even more. Keep the soil moist but not dripping wet, and sprouts will likely form in a couple weeks. After the sprouts emerge, prepare them for planting as you would in the water method.

Growing Conditions

Sweet potatoes love warm weather. Transplant them outside after all danger of frost has passed and the soil temperature consistently reaches above 65°F. If you have colder summers or a shorter growing season, cover your soil with a black tarp or woven black plastic mulch for a couple weeks before you plant your sweet potato slips. That step will help warm the soil faster when temperatures can stay stubbornly cold despite the air warming. Remove the tarp before planting or, if using woven plastic mulch, punch holes in which to plant the slips; keep it on throughout the growing season for added warmth. After transplanting them, covering your sweet potato plants with row cover will give you a few extra weeks of growing time and increase the air temperature around the plants. In the fall, as the weather cools, you can put the row cover on again to keep them growing just a bit longer.

Slips purchased online will probably be wrapped in paper or plastic and look a bit sad. That's OK! As long as you get them into soil right away and give them proper moisture, they'll perk up quickly. If you can't plant them soon after they arrive or the weather is still too cold, keep them in a warm, shaded place. Check the roots every day and spray them with water if they dry out, but don't submerge them in water or get the leaves wet. Sticking the root ends of your slips in a shallow tray of potting soil or damp newspaper

strips will keep them fresh if you need to store them for more than a week.

When the conditions are right to get your plants in the ground, plant your sweet potato slips in rich, loamy soil 12 to 18 inches apart and deep enough that most of the slip is underground, with just the top set of leaves above the soil. Plant them in the evening or on an overcast day and water them well after planting. Keep the plants well-watered for the first couple weeks until they are established and growing new leaves. After that point, they should receive the standard inch per week from rain or irrigation.

Sweet potato vines sprawl quickly to cover the ground, so they'll shade out weeds as long as they have a head start. They can also work as a "living mulch" around the base of taller plants, similar to squash.

Pests and Diseases

Deer love sweet potato leaves and will go to a lot of trouble to munch on these plants. Even with a sturdy garden fence, we cover our sweet potatoes right after we plant them and remove the cover only after they have established and become less attractive to pests, usually after about a month. This method also helps disguise them from other critters, including rabbits and voles, which are much harder to keep out with fencing.

In the Northeast, our sweet potatoes have had very little issue with insect damage, though generalist pests, such as aphids and whiteflies, still pose a problem right after planting or during drought. If you water your plants well and cover them while they're getting established, you likely won't have many problems with pests on your sweet potatoes.

Sweet potatoes benefit from a lot of water, but they are prone to root rot if the ground stays saturated for too long, so well-draining soil is a must. Before planting sweet potatoes in heavier clay soils, digging in lots of compost or growing a deep-rooted cover crop can help them grow.

Our Favorite Varieties

At the supermarket, you'll find the classic Covington and Beauregard sweet potatoes with brown skin and orange flesh. These classics are great, but there are many other varieties out there with their own unique flavor profiles. The Evangeline variety tastes super sweet and has lots of beta-carotene but with somewhat lower yields than the first two cultivars. You also can find sweet potatoes of excellent stock but no variety name in grocery stores. We still dream of a purple-fleshed sweet potato we bought from our local food co-op many years ago. We grew slips from it on our windowsill—they were highly productive and tasted exceedingly sweet and tender. We encourage you to grow a tried-and-true variety for the bulk of your crop but mix in some experimental varieties for fun. You might discover the perfect one for your garden.

Harvest and Preservation

Because they are a warm-weather crop, sweet potatoes will not continue growing once the first frost arrives. Here in zone 6B, we usually wait until the first light frost (30°F to 32°F), which kills the aboveground leaves but doesn't harm the soil-insulated roots. Absolutely harvest them before a hard freeze (below 28°F), which may damage the sweet potatoes and make them unsuitable for storage. After the first light frost, digging sweet potatoes can feel incredibly exciting because it's impossible to know how the harvest will go until you stick a spade in the soil.

When harvesting, use a pitchfork to avoid slicing through the roots and dig 1 to 2 feet deep. In our second year of farming, we grew sweet potatoes in large raised beds, hoping the increased drainage and warmth would help. In the fall, we pulled the vines and were dismayed to see not a single sweet potato underneath. We stood there, confused, wondering how we were going to fill our CSA orders that week, when Silvan spied a little chunk of pinky-orange something peeking up from the soil. With a little elbow grease, a sweet potato roughly the size of her head popped out! What followed was the best sweet potato harvest we've ever had, and we might have missed it completely by not digging deep enough!

When harvesting, handle your sweet potatoes gently. Their skin is still tender and easily damaged at this point. Gently brush off large pieces of dirt, but don't wash or scrub them. Eat any small and skinny ones or those with obvious cuts and bruises because they won't store well. For the rest to last longer in storage, they need to cure. Sit them in a warm, humid place for a few weeks so their skin hardens and any small cuts or scrapes heal over. During curing, the flesh also firms up and sweetens. After curing, you should store them somewhere cool and dry. We keep ours in baskets in the basement (next to our dehumidifier, since Pittsburgh basements are notoriously damp).

SWEET POTATO CASSEROLE WITH HONEY ROASTED PECANS

This sweet and savory dish is reminiscent of the classic dish eaten alongside turkey and green beans at Thanksgiving dinner, but honey roasted pecans take it to a whole new level. It works great as a side for a rich, hearty dinner or even as a meal on its own!

4 to 6 sweet potatoes, about
    4 cups chopped

2 eggs

1 cup pecans

½ cup honey, divided

6 tablespoons unsalted butter,
    room temperature, divided

½ teaspoon salt, plus 1 pinch

1. Peel the sweet potatoes and chop them into 1-inch cubes.

2. In a medium pot, add the sweet potatoes, cover them with water, place the pot over medium-high heat, and bring it to a boil. Cook until the sweet potatoes soften, 10 to 15 minutes.

3. Meanwhile, preheat the oven to 350°F, lightly beat the eggs, and chop the pecans. Set aside.

4. When the sweet potatoes have finished boiling, transfer them to a baking dish and mash them.

5. Add the eggs, ¼ cup of honey, 4 tablespoons of butter, and ½ teaspoon of salt and stir to combine well.

6. In a small mixing bowl, combine the chopped pecans, the remaining ¼ cup of honey, the remaining 2 tablespoons of butter, and the pinch of salt.

7. Top the mashed sweet potato mixture with the pecan mixture.

8. Bake until the pecan topping begins to brown, about 30 minutes.

SWEET POTATO GRATIN

On frost-tinged days, with winter hanging in the air, making this starchy, rich, satisfyingly sweet dish perfectly celebrates a good harvest—or serves as comforting consolation for a bad one. It's also a great way to use up any sweet potatoes with nicks or bruises that won't keep well in storage. This is a great meal to make and freeze for later.

Butter or olive oil for greasing

2 or 3 sweet potatoes, about 2 pounds total

1 large bunch fresh thyme, about ½ cup, plus a few leaves for topping

1 small bunch sage, fresh or dried, about ¼ cup, plus a few leaves for topping

1 cup grated Parmesan cheese

1 cup heavy cream

2 cloves garlic

1 teaspoon salt

1 teaspoon freshly ground black pepper, plus more for topping

1. Preheat the oven to 375°F and grease a baking dish with butter or olive oil.

2. With a mandoline, slice the sweet potatoes into thin disks. In the prepared baking dish, place enough sweet potato slices to form one layer. They should overlap slightly, but don't stack them atop one another.

3. Chop the thyme and sage and, in a small mixing bowl, stir to combine with the Parmesan cheese.

4. Sprinkle a third of the cheese mixture evenly on the first layer of sweet potatoes.

5. Add another layer of sweet potato slices and more of the cheese mixture until you use all the sweet potato slices.

6. In a small mixing bowl, add the heavy cream.

7. Mince the garlic and add it, along with the salt, pepper, and any remaining cheese mixture, to the heavy cream. Stir to combine.

8. Slowly pour the seasoned cream mixture over the sweet potatoes. Top with a few sage and thyme leaves and more freshly ground black pepper.

9. Cook until the cheese bubbles and browns and the potatoes have become tender, about 45 minutes.

TOMATOES

Per Pound
CALORIES: 99   **CARBS:** 17.3 g   **PROTEIN:** 3.2 g   **FAT:** 1.9 g
IMPORTANT MICRONUTRIENTS: lycopene, vitamin C

We probably all know at this point that a ripe, homegrown tomato is an entirely different beast than the stiff, anemic spheres sold at most grocery stores. Commercial tomatoes are bred for their color, shipping ability, and not much else. Guy Clark famously sang that there are "only two things that money can't buy, and that's true love and homegrown tomatoes." You can get close with tomatoes bought at peak season from the local farmers' market, but it'll cost you. In our area, heirloom tomatoes generally sell for $5 or more per pound.

As a country, we have quite a love affair with tomatoes. In 2019, estimates of fresh tomatoes produced in or imported to the United States clocked in at 6.7 billion pounds—more than 20 pounds per person—and that number doesn't count the tomatoes used in tomato sauce, ketchup, and other processed tomato products. At the farm Silvan runs for her day job, the most frequently asked question she hears every spring is: "When will you have ripe tomatoes?"

Tomatoes are now considered a foundational ingredient of many cuisines throughout the world, but they come from humble beginnings. Growing wild in the Andes Mountains of South America, they began as weedy nightshade plants with tiny, pea-sized fruit. Historians don't know exactly when the people of Mesoamerica first domesticated them, but the Mexica people grew several varieties for their cuisine. During Spanish colonization of South America, the tomato was introduced to Europe, where it was first grown mainly for ornamental purposes. Europeans recognized its physical similarity to belladonna, a deadly nightshade native to Europe and Asia, and suspected this new fruit of being poisonous, which of course it isn't. It eventually caught on and soon became an essential ingredient in European, Middle Eastern, and North African food.

What tomatoes lack in calories, they make up for in flavor, versatility, and micronutrients. We always make room in our garden for tomatoes because they play a part in so many of our favorite meals: salsas, stews, chilis, ragùs, and more. After our staple crops—corn, beans, squash, and potatoes—tomatoes are probably the ingredient in our pantry we reach for most often. They can preserve excellently, and processed tomatoes contain up to 150 percent more lycopene than their raw counterparts. Lycopene is a powerful antioxidant that gives tomatoes their red color and, according to some studies, eating it regularly may help lower the risks of cancer and heart disease. Every year we preserve quarts of tomato sauce, tomato paste, and whole tomatoes. We also use tomatoes in other canned goods, including salsa, chutney, and ketchup.

Tomatoes are a little more finicky than some of the other crops in this book. A lot of first-time gardeners become discouraged when they start growing tomatoes, that most classic of home-grown fruit, and come up against problems like poor growth, disease pressure, or splitting fruit. Read on and we'll explain how to prevent or tackle these challenges and why we think tomatoes are well worth the effort!

Seed Starting

Start your seeds indoors about a month before you plan to transplant them. Tomatoes don't like cold weather, so wait until after the average last frost in your growing zone to transplant them outdoors.

Growing your own tomatoes from seed rather than buying seedlings at a nursery means selecting from thousands of heirloom varieties. They are one of the most diverse crops in the world, with an estimated 10,000 existing cultivated varieties. Trying to grow them all would overwhelm anyone, so start by asking local folks at the farmers' market or friends who garden for some of their favorites that grow well in your area. You can usually buy tomato seeds in quantities of 10, so it's easy to try a few varieties each year and trade with friends.

At a high level, tomato plants fall into two types: determinate and indeterminate. Determinate plants grow to a certain height, then produce all their fruit at once. This category works ideally for sauce or some other processing project for which you want a big pile all at once. If you want a consistent supply throughout the season, focus on indeterminate varieties, which grow and produce fruit over time until they succumb to disease or winter. We grow a mix of the two so we can eat fresh tomatoes from indeterminate varieties all summer and harvest a big pile from our determinate tomatoes to can for sauce. Most seed companies specify the type in the variety description.

It's easy to start tomatoes from seed using the principles in our Seed Starting chapter (page 20). Because the seeds are tiny, you'll only need to press a little hole, about ¼ inch deep, into your potting soil. We usually put two seeds in each well of a 72-cell seedling tray to ensure that at least one sprouts. If they both sprout, we cull the smaller one after they emerge to give the bigger one room to grow.

When your tomato seedlings reach about 3 inches tall and have a couple of true leaves, consider up-potting them to larger containers so their root systems can continue developing. Before transplanting your seedlings outside, harden them off for about three days. Tomatoes have delicate leaves that are very susceptible to sun scald, so transplanting them without hardening them off can result in big patches of white and brown damage on the leaves. They will likely recover if they survive the initial shock, but it's always better to prevent it in the first place. Tomatoes also benefit from good airflow as seedlings to create strong, stocky stems that will resist breaking in the wind.

Growing Conditions

When it's time to transplant your tomatoes, plant them deep in the soil. Tomatoes have adventitious roots, meaning that, if conditions are right, they can send roots out anywhere along the stem. Inspect your tomato seedlings closely and you'll see tiny translucent hairs along the central stem. If buried in the soil and given adequate moisture, all these hairs can become roots, which will give your plants a strong anchor and jump-start the process of developing a healthy root system.

Tomatoes need full sun, at least six hours a day, and you should leave about 1½ feet of space between each plant. Tomatoes can grow very tall, so make sure you have a plan in place to support them and put them in a spot where they won't shade out other sun-loving plants once they get to full size. Tomatoes work well for container gardening if you have large enough containers, at least 5 gallons each. Plants grown in containers are more likely to dry out than in-ground plants, and tomatoes require a lot of water. If you do plant them in pots, water them consistently and give them a healthy dose of compost to support them throughout the season.

When your tomatoes reach about a foot tall, trellis them to keep them from flopping over. Although we typically think of tomatoes as an upright plant, they naturally grow on the ground as a vine. If you live in a dry area and lay down some landscape fabric to keep them from making contact with the soil, you can get away with growing them naturally. If you live somewhere that gets a good amount of rainfall, your tomatoes will require trellising, or they'll more or less rot on the ground.

There are a couple ways to trellis tomatoes, but our preferred method is called the "Florida weave." This simple process entails placing two stakes on either end of your row of tomatoes and wrapping the stakes and plants with twine to prop up the vines. Start with one layer of twine and, every couple weeks, when the plants start to topple over, add another layer of twine 6 inches to a foot above the last. If you use this method, indeterminate tomatoes can become very heavy, so invest in some solid metal T-posts and use strong twine. To provide enough support, space your stakes about every five to six plants and pound the T-posts at least a foot into the ground.

You can also stake each tomato individually and tie them higher and higher up the stake as new growth emerges, but this method requires more labor and pruning than the weave style

A tomato sucker growing at a 45-degree angle from where a branch joins the stem

of trellis. A lot of garden centers and hardware stores sell tomato cages, but we only recommend them for small determinate tomatoes. Most indeterminates grow much taller than the largest cages.

Tomatoes are particularly susceptible to fungal disease, so thinning their canopy to allow for good air flow is very important. Regular pruning keeps the plants from overwhelming their trellis and lets you see and harvest ripe fruit more easily.

One of the best methods to keep them from getting too busy is to "sucker" them. Suckering is a very simple process once you know what you're looking at. Each tomato plant has a primary stem, and along that stem are branches, leaves, and "suckers." The branches and leaves grow at a 90-degree angle to the main stem, and the sucker usually grows at a 45-degree angle from what we like to call the armpit of this junction. Either snap off the suckers when they're small and tender or, if you find them when they've grown a little bigger, cut them off with a sharp knife or pruners. In shorter growing seasons, as is the case in most of the United States, it's important to limit the plant's vegetative growth by removing suckers, which helps the plant focus on ripening tomatoes, resulting in more fruit.

Pests and Diseases

Tomatoes are subject to a large number of pests and diseases. It seems that everybody—fungi and bacteria included—likes tomatoes! It would be difficult (and boring) to catalog every single pest and disease that could impact a tomato plant, so our suggestion is to familiarize yourself with some of the most common ones here and don't worry about the rest. If something starts happening to your tomato plants that you haven't seen before, research the specific symptoms on your local university extension website to learn how to manage the problem, or consult with other local gardeners. But don't let the number of possible issues scare you from growing tomatoes. They are a fun and very rewarding crop to grow,

and we have great success with them every year, even with less-than-ideal conditions.

Tomato hornworms (*Manduca quinquemaculata*) are the scourge of many tomato growers in North America. These massive green and white caterpillars camouflage well and can defoliate an entire tomato plant in just days. Luckily, parasitoid wasps like *Cotesia congregata* use tomato hornworms as one of their primary hosts, laying their eggs under the caterpillar's skin so that their larvae can hatch and eat the insides of the hornworm as they grow. (Nature can be brutal!) If you find white cocoons hanging from a hornworm's back, it has essentially become a zombie and no longer poses a threat to your plants. If that's the case, leave them in the garden so the wasp larvae emerge and parasitize any other hornworms on your tomatoes. If you find hornworms without the parasites, simply pull them off the plant and smush them or feed them to

A tomato hornworm colonized by parasitoid wasps

some chickens if you have them. If you're facing a true infestation and handpicking isn't a viable option, the organic pesticide Bt works effectively against them.

Armyworms, which are smaller than hornworms, are gray or black with a light stripe running down their sides. They go after tomato fruit, usually tunneling through them before the fruit ripens. You can handpick them or control them with Bt.

Aphids and whiteflies—both tiny, sap-sucking insects—commonly attack tomato plants. They seem to pose more of a problem for new seedlings, especially if the seedlings weren't particularly healthy to begin with. The best way to control these pests is by growing healthy seedlings, hardening them off well before transplanting to the garden, and watering well. Stressed plants are more likely to be harmed by aphids and whiteflies, while sturdier plants can weather their damage and bounce back quickly after conditions change and the pests leave. You can also cultivate habitat in your garden for their natural predators, including ladybugs and lacewings.

In the hot, humid conditions of the eastern United States where we garden, fungal diseases represent enemy number one for growing tomatoes. Many commercial tomato growers plant their crops in high tunnels or greenhouses, where they can control the moisture and keep fungal diseases at bay more effectively. For home gardeners, preventing crowded foliage through pruning and suckering will go a long way to

Yellow spots on tomato leaves

reducing disease pressure. Many tomato diseases originate in the soil, meaning that fungal spores overwinter in affected soil until they make their way onto new plants to multiply when conditions are right. To keep a good barrier between the soil and the lower leaves of our plants, we mulch our tomatoes with straw or a heavy layer of compost.

Most tomato diseases, while unsightly, won't actually kill your plants before you can harvest from them, but they can reduce your yield. Keep an eye out for the beginning stages of disease, such as dark brown or yellow spots on the leaves, and remove them quickly to prevent them from spreading. Before winter hits, your tomatoes will likely succumb to a fungal disease like late blight, but that's totally normal. If you've already harvested a good pile of tomatoes, don't worry about it too much. Just remember to remove all your spent tomato plants from the garden and hot compost them to prevent the fungal disease from spreading during the following season.

Our Favorite Varieties

For fresh eating, you can't beat the classic heirloom flavor of a Cherokee Purple tomato. These large slicers make an unbeatable tomato sandwich and often produce more tomatoes than one family knows what to do with. Another of our favorites, Jaune Flamme ("yellow flame" in French), has a rich, tangy flavor. It starts fruiting early in the season and often remains disease-free for us all summer. We grow a few of these plants every year for fresh eating in salads or salsa.

Sungold cherry tomatoes probably are the closest a vegetable—yes, technically a fruit, but you know what we mean—has ever come to candy. They have an incredibly high sugar content and do really well in salads or roasted

tomato dishes, though we grow them mostly for snacking straight from the plant, warmed by the sun, while we work in the garden. If you have kids, we definitely suggest growing some of these to instill a lifelong love of tomatoes in them. Sungolds tend to split, so harvest regularly. A newer variety, Honeydrop, tastes similar but is less prone to splitting, which makes it a good option for growing in an area with heavy rainfall.

San Marzano, a wonderful paste-style heirloom, is excellent for that classic tomato sauce flavor. We cook them down into sauce and paste or dry them in the sun. We also can them whole to use in winter stews. Another variety of paste tomato, the hybrid Roma variety Monica, is a compact determinate plant that is perfect for growing in containers or small spaces and still produces a great yield of tomatoes for preserving.

Harvest and Preservation

Depending on how many plants you grow, you will likely end up with a *big* surplus on your counter and need some ways to put them away for the winter.

The simplest method of preserving tomatoes is to cut them up, put them on a sheet pan with some garlic, onions, herbs, and olive oil, and roast them until they start to caramelize. After they've cooled, pour them in freezer bags and freeze them until you're ready to use them in pasta dishes, pizza, soup, etc. We love this method for cherry tomatoes, which aren't ideal for preservation recipes that involve peeling or chopping!

Sun-drying tomatoes is another simple method of preservation. But if you live in a cool or humid climate, you might need the help of a dehydrator to get them completely dry. We like to slice Roma tomatoes in half, sprinkle them with salt to start drawing out the moisture, and

if the weather is cooperating, sit them on trays in the sun for a few days. Then we pop them into our dehydrator to finish the job. After they've become dry and brittle and you can't see any moisture when pressing a fingernail into them, they're ready to store. We keep ours in airtight Mason jars in our pantry or layer them in oil and store them in the fridge for later cooking.

To preserve canned tomatoes, we recommend following tested recipes like those on the website for the National Center for Home Food Preservation, which has excellent recommendations for preserving shelf-stable food safely and avoiding potential contamination. This is our primary method of preserving tomatoes for the winter. Each year, we can several quarts each of tomato sauce, paste, salsa, and whole tomatoes, all using recipes from the NCHFP. If you don't have enough tomatoes at one time to fill a canner, put them in bags in the freezer until you have enough. Defrost them, drain the excess water, remove the skins, and cook them down into sauce or, if you prefer, can them whole. As the tomatoes defrost, the skins will slip off easily, which means you can skip the time- and energy-intensive step in most canning recipes that requires submerging the tomatoes in boiling water to remove the skins. Of course, if you have the freezer space, you can skip canning altogether. But water-bath canning is a great skill to learn if you want to eat from your garden year-round.

GARDEN SALSA

In late summer, when everything feels hot and sticky, the *last* thing we want to do is turn on the stove. So fresh salsa makes a perfect snack. Adding some beans or other protein can even make it a meal. Roma tomatoes provide bulk and sturdiness, while heirloom tomatoes bring their signature sweetness and depth of flavor. Letting the tomatoes drain in a colander before making the salsa will keep the salsa from turning into soup. If you don't have or don't want to use limes, substitute 3 or 4 tablespoons of apple cider vinegar.

---

3 Roma tomatoes (about 1 pound)

3 or 4 medium heirloom tomatoes of choice (about 1 pound)

1 teaspoon salt

1 clove garlic

2 jalapeño peppers

1 small red onion

Juice of 2 limes

½ cup chopped cilantro

1 pinch dried oregano

Salt and pepper

1. Chop all the tomatoes into 1-inch chunks, scraping out the seeds as you go, and place the chunks in a colander over a bowl.

2. Sprinkle the tomatoes with the salt and mix. Let the tomatoes drain for 10 to 15 minutes, stirring occasionally to release the excess moisture.

3. Chop the garlic, jalapeño peppers, and onion. For milder salsa, omit the jalapeño seeds and ribs. For a hotter one, include the seeds and use a hotter pepper, such as serrano or habanero.

4. Add the chopped vegetables to the tomatoes and stir to combine.

5. Add the lime juice, cilantro, and oregano and mix well.

6. Add salt and pepper to taste and more lime juice if necessary. Serve immediately with Corn Tortillas (page 96). In an airtight container in the fridge, the salsa will keep well for 3 to 4 days.

TABBOULI

Tabbouli is incredibly popular in the Middle East, and it's no wonder why. Fresh vegetables chopped into bite-sized pieces and bright, tangy dressing perfectly accompany any summer meal. Each region has its own take on the dish, and this is our version of what Jordan's family has made for generations, modified slightly with ingredients that are easy to grow and harvest where we live in Pennsylvania. Bulgur wheat is traditional, but cornmeal makes an interesting, equally delicious substitute that we can grow abundantly in our backyard.

---

1 cup water

3 lemons

½ cup medium cornmeal

2 teaspoons sea salt, divided

⅓ cup extra virgin olive oil plus an additional splash

3 or 4 medium tomatoes, such as Roma

2 medium cucumbers

1 large bunch curly parsley

1 large clove garlic

1 bunch green onions

1. Boil the water and juice the lemons for 2 ounces of fresh juice.

2. In a heat-safe container, add the boiling water, cornmeal, 1 teaspoon of salt, 1 ounce of lemon juice, and a splash of olive oil. Stir to combine, cover, and set aside to cool.

3. Dice the tomatoes and cucumbers into ¼-inch pieces and add them to a large mixing bowl with the remaining teaspoon of salt.

4. Stem the parsley and chop it finely or use a food processor. Mince the garlic and green onions.

5. Add the parsley, green onions, and cooked cornmeal to the tomatoes and cucumbers and mix well.

6. In a small mixing bowl, add the olive oil, the remaining ounce of lemon juice, and the garlic and stir to combine.

7. Add the dressing to the salad and toss to coat evenly.

8. Taste and adjust salt or acid if necessary. You can eat it right away, but it tastes even better after the flavors mingle in the fridge for a few hours.

RESOURCES

Seed Companies

Alliance of Native Seedkeepers

Botanical Interests

Fedco Seeds

High Mowing Organic Seeds

Johnny's Selected Seeds

Seed Savers Exchange

Sow True Seed

Truelove Seeds

Books about Farming and Gardening

The Ecological Farm: A Minimalist No-Till, No-Spray, Selective-Weeding, Grow-Your-Own-Fertilizer System for Organic Agriculture by Helen Atthowe

Organic Mushroom Farming and Mycoremediation: Simple to Advanced and Experimental Techniques for Indoor and Outdoor Cultivation by Tradd Cotter

The Organic No-Till Farming Revolution: High-Production Methods for Small-Scale Farmers by Andrew Mefferd

Books about Cooking and Preserving

The Art of Fermentation: An In-Depth Exploration of Essential Concepts and Processes from around the World by Sandor Ellix Katz

Canning for a New Generation: Bold, Fresh Flavors for the Modern Pantry by Liana Krissoff

New Native Kitchen: Celebrating Modern Recipes of the American Indian by Freddie Bitsoie and James O. Fraioli

Six Seasons: A New Way with Vegetables by Joshua McFadden and Martha Holmberg

Other Websites and Online Resources

American Community Gardening Association map, www.communitygarden.org/garden

National Center for Home Food Preservation, nchfp.uga.edu/

INDEX